This book is due for return on or before the last date shown below.

To adults in the workplace who want to be treated as such

Cover design: Paul McCarthy

Published by John Wiley & Sons, Inc., Hoboken, New Jersey.
Published simultaneously in Canada.

For general information about our other products and services, please contact our Customer Care Department within the United States at (800) 762-2974, outside the United States at (317) 572-3993 or fax (317) 572-4002.

Wiley publishes in a variety of print and electronic formats and by print-on-demand. Some material included with standard print versions of this book may not be included in e-books or in print-on-demand. If this book refers to media such as a CD or DVD that is not included in the version you purchased, you may download this material at http://booksupport.wiley.com. For more information about Wiley products, visit www.wiley.com.

Library of Congress Cataloging-in-Publication Data:

Ressler, Cali.
   Why Managing Sucks and How to Fix It: A Results-Only Guide to Taking Control of Work, Not People/Cali Ressler and Jody Thompson.
   ISBN: 978-1-118-42636-4 (cloth); ISBN: 978-1-118-55934-5 (ebk);
   ISBN: 978-1-118-55928-4 (ebk); ISBN: 978-1-118-55924-6 (ebk)
   1. Personnel management. 2. Quality of work life. I. Thompson, Jody. II. Title.
   HF5549
   658.3–dc23
                                                        2012044789

Printed in the United States of America
10 9 8 7 6 5 4 3 2 1

WHY MANAGING SUCKS AND HOW TO FIX IT

A RESULTS-ONLY GUIDE TO TAKING CONTROL OF WORK, NOT PEOPLE

CALI RESSLER
JODY THOMPSON

WILEY

John Wiley & Sons, Inc.

Contents

Acknowledgments

A lot has happened since we set out to change the broken system called "work" back in 2003. Each day, more and more organizations are joining the revolution, reinventing their work cultures—really going *beyond telework*—to create an environment where people can truly thrive. A place where work is no longer a four-letter word. A place where managed flexibility around 9–5 office hours is so last century. A place where everyone is accountable to the work and is intrinsically motivated to succeed. A place that we were told time and time again couldn't really exist—utopia?—and we've proved *does* exist.

So to the people in organizations (some mentioned in this book) who have courageously worked with us to ignite their workplaces, you are the leaders of the future of work; it's not easy to be the first to buck the system, but it does put you in a unique position to change the lives of many people to come and sets you on a trajectory that puts you ahead of the productivity and innovation curve.

To Adrianna Johnson, Christine Moore, and the rest of the team at John Wiley & Sons, Inc.—thank you. Your encouragement and gentle nudging along the way helped us shape the second phase of our journey into an actionable tool for managers. We're proud of what we've accomplished together.

And to our team at CultureRx: every day we are thankful for you. You continue to be energized by making it part of your own personal mission to make sure that work doesn't suck for people. You get up every day and dedicate yourselves to making global change happen one person at a time.

Cali's Special Thanks

To Trystan, Jackson, Keaton, and McKenna—my kids who keep me going on this journey because I want them to love not only what they do when they grow up but be in control of how they do it. Every day, I am more and more proud of you. Yes, Mom is a *real* author—and someday you'll read this book and think, "Oh, *this* is what she was writing!"

To my husband, Marty, my perfect match. You and me—always and forever.

To my parents, Jose and Heidi Gaibor, who support me in everything I do. Time to enjoy life even more now that you're nearing retirement, Pops, and time will *really* be your own. Crazy that the father of the cocreator of ROWE had to endure decades at an organization that focused on time, hours, and everything that didn't matter—definitely provided me with even more sense of purpose to carry on. Congratulations on the traction you're making in opening some minds little by little, day by day. Sit back, relax, and grab a Corona. You deserve it!

To my grandfather, Bob Hoeppner, who knew that teaching me to never give up as a young girl would be an important lesson that would carry me far in life.

To my brother, Jesse Gaibor. As far as siblings go, you really are the best, and I appreciate your advice as I continue on this journey. Wouldn't trade you or Tara for anything.

To my in-laws—Adam, Joyce, Mandy, Emeric, Monty, and Natalie—thank you for your support in everything I take on. Enjoy this second book!

To friends who are there to listen, laugh, and enjoy life as it unfolds. I appreciate every one of you and your encouragement of my adventures. I look forward to many, many more years of good times.

Jody's Special Thanks

To my sons, Colin and Elliot. Every day I wake up and am simply amazed that I get to claim to be your mom! I am so proud of what you're accomplishing in your lives. There will always be roadblocks and frustrations along the way, but what you *do* does make a difference. And who you *are* is more than I could have ever hoped for.

To my parents, George and Beverly Hartzell. You may not always understand why I do the things I do, or where I get some of my crazy ideas, but you're always there to cheer me on. Thank you for your love and support—and most importantly, for believing in me.

And to my fiancé, Mike Huba. I've been swept off my feet by your enthusiasm for life! Thank you for showing me through actions, not just words, that a truly loving relationship is possible, that being myself is exactly what I should be.

To Alex Huba. Your dedication to serving our country and defending freedom is remarkable. You are truly a blessing in my life.

And to my dear friend Pia-Kim Genung. Without your support over the past couple of years, I would have taken up residence in the loony bin. Thank you for always being there to listen, give me new perspectives, and share a great bottle of wine.

Introduction

Back in 2003, my business partner, Cali Ressler, and I were employees in the human resources (HR) department at Best Buy, Co., Inc., where we got the crazy idea that organizations could trust their people to do their work and live their lives without having to intervene or "manage" them. We believed that giving people what they really wanted—*complete autonomy* to manage all of the demands in their lives—could actually be successful. Businesses would prosper. People would be happier. And, we had faith—faith that people would not only *want* to but *would* do the right thing. ROWE—Results-Only Work Environment—was born out of this faith.

Since then, we've validated the fact that this simple notion was, indeed, correct. When you treat people like adults, they act like adults. When people are treated like children, they act out. And we've proved that organizations can trust their employees to own their work without outdated HR policies regarding office hours, time off, dress code, inclement weather, and the like. The notion that "Some people just need more structure" was exposed for what it really is: another way of saying, "I don't know how to effectively manage the *work*, so now I'm going to manage *you*."

One of our clients, Kyle Pederson, owner of Learner's Edge, whose organization offers leading-edge, thought-provoking, versatile graduate credit for teachers, said,

> As a manager, I need to manage the work, not the people. [Doing so allows me to] enable my employees to have control—*they* get to manage their lives. The majority of their waking hours are no longer dictated by a boss—they are no longer scheduled for 40 specific hours every week, and then made to somehow fit the rest of their busy lives around it. A healthy work/life balance is absolutely critical—but can only be accomplished when employees manage their time. And [they can't do this] when I, as their boss, require them to be in a specific location at a specific time for 8+ hours per day, 50+ weeks per year. In the end, a ROWE results in much more balanced, happy employees who feel more empowered and in control of their own lives. What manager wouldn't want that?

Our first book, published in June 2008, *Why Work Sucks and How to Fix It: No Schedules, No Meetings, No Joke—The Simple Change That Can Make Your Job Terrific*, was the manifesto of a ROWE. It attacked the relevance of the "everyone on deck" approach, and opened up the possibility of "everyone on *point*." It laid out the problem with work: it's not the work that sucks; it's the *way* we're forced to do the work that sucks. And it gave our readers insight into how to fix it. It positioned a ROWE as the future of work and not some silly flexible work program from the twentieth century or a sneaky way to give the keys to the kingdom to us slackers.

This book is going to slow it down and break it up a bit. We'll do a deeper dive into specific practices that managers can experiment with to update their current style. We'll examine tired, old methods and give you tools with which to replace them. And, once and for all, we're going to show you how a ROWE goes beyond the tele-work mentality and how it works for *every* job in *every* industry. In fact we'll take you there with examples from the social and public sectors. You'll not only hear it from us, but from leaders who have boldly and coura-geously ventured into adopting an authentic ROWE through training by our company, CultureRx. Too many meetings? We've got you covered. Can't figure out why your employees are leaving, even though you think you've got top-notch benefits and rewards? We get it. Still believe some people need more structure? *Read this book!*

And by the way, there's no *version* of a ROWE. Look out for the fakers that give a few people flexibility and claim that they're a ROWE organization. You'll get in and find out that results aren't clear, judgment about how people spend their time is rampant, and employees are even still hearing that they can't be in a ROWE for whatever lame-o reason management comes up with. You're either a ROWE, or you're not. Period.

An authentic ROWE is, in its essence, a contem-porary work culture built on the foundation that we hire people for clear, measurable results. It's why they have *jobs*. Just "putting in time" doesn't cut it in a ROWE.

Filling time doesn't cut it. Measuring time doesn't cut it. Showing up to work doesn't cut it. Time really has no relevance unless it's used to manage deadlines, due dates, deliverables, and such—that is, the *work*. If a functional or client meeting starts at 1:00 PM, then 1:00 PM has relevance. But if I come into the office at 8:15 AM instead of 8:00 AM and am producing results and not missing anything that *is* time sensitive, then 8:15 AM has no relevance whatsoever.

Flexible work programs have simply reinforced the notion that time has relevance. And a ROWE is not a flexible work program; in fact, comparing it to one is nuts, because they are as different as night and day. Just by definition, if people are going to be flexible, they need to be flexible *around something*, and that something is office hours and the physical office. "I'm working from home tomorrow" (that is, teleworking), says I should be in the office (default), but I'm going to be at home (flexible). "I work four 10-hour days with Fridays off" says I should be in the office on Fridays like everyone else (default), but I'm putting in my time in four days instead of five (flexible). "My hours are Monday through Thursday from 7:30 AM to 4:30 PM and Fridays from 8 AM to 4 PM" says normal office hours are 8 AM to 5 PM Monday through Friday (default), but I have my own personal schedule that's different (flexible).

"Our research suggests that a ROWE brings real benefits to employees in terms of their work/life fit and their health and well-being, while also benefiting the company by reducing turnover," says Erin Kelly, professor of sociology for the University of Minnesota.

She continues, "We believe that ROWE's collective approach—the insistence on changing the culture rather than offering limited flexibility to just a few people—is key to employees' improved ability to manage their whole lives in a healthy and happy way."

Of course, we understand why people *think* they want flexibility. And we don't blame them. They just want *some* control over their lives, no matter how little. They feel a tiny bit of flexibility takes them to a happy place where work and life live in harmony. But then they find out that what they thought was a wonderful accommodation was really a whole new level of management control and coworker judgment.

First, *flexible schedule* is an oxymoron. By definition, there's nothing flexible about a *schedule*. The second you get your new flexible schedule, life happens. All of a sudden you need to go to the dentist at 2:00 in the afternoon on Wednesday when Friday is your day off. Boy, that puts you in a pickle. Now you have to inform your manager you're leaving early or even worse, you may need to get permission to go off schedule. You feel naughty and even guilty, because your manager was so nice to *allow* you that flexible schedule in the first place— and now you seem to be taking advantage of it.

And second, the minute you get that flexible schedule, everyone else wants one. How come *you* got one? Oh, you have kids. I wish I had kids. You've been here two years, so you've earned it. The manager who decided your job can be flexible, but not mine. And countless other reasons arise. Flexibility programs bless some people with an accommodation, but not all people.

And it's up to the manager's discretion. You can only hope to suck up enough.

Third, being on a flexible schedule is like having a neon sign on your forehead flashing, "My priorities are out of whack!" or "I'm not as dedicated to work as the rest of the team" or "My career is taking a backseat to my life." Oops. You just tripped and fell a few rungs down on the career ladder. Oh, you silly, flexible work schedule!

A ROWE goes where no "so last century" flexibility program will ever go by leveling the playing field. After all, who can argue with the fact that people need to achieve agreed-upon, measurable results to get a paycheck? There are a million arguments a day about who gets to be flexible, who's earned flexibility, or who should be deemed "able to be flexible." These arguments waste the time of managers who *should* be focusing on other things—namely, making it clear to each person what he or she was hired to do and how to measure it. Yet these managers are spending precious time managing something that will never be fairly managed, at least, that's how the people wanting flexibility see it.

A ROWE gives each and every person complete control over their time, and not just some of it—*all* of it. That's right, all 168 hours a week. And we've learned that when people have complete control over all of their time, they begin to use it wisely to optimize every aspect of their lives, including work. They stop wasting company time, filling it with nonsense, and playing the crazy time games.

That's why the definition of a ROWE is simple yet powerful. Each person is free to do *whatever* they want, *whenever* they want—as long as they get the work done.

Let's break it down: Each person is free to manage his or her life using common sense. And that means stepping up to the plate or slacking off. Each person is free to work in harmony with other people or not. And each person is free to engage or disengage. Adding *to do whatever they want, whenever they want* adds an important dimension, because *to do* includes everything in my life. There are things I *need* to do—grocery shop, pick up the kids from day care, do laundry, sleep, *work*—and there are things I *want* to do—exercise, hang out with friends, spend time on my hobbies, and volunteer. Then, to really make it fun, throw in "as long as the work gets done." That's the whole point. People must do the work; that's why the paycheck exists. So if I choose to slack off, to not work in harmony and instead disengage, then I'm not performing. And I don't get to keep my job.

This simple definition of a ROWE is potent enough to cause rioting on Management Lane. It's how we knew deep inside—and have seen play out time and time again—that people really aren't clear at all about what the work really is and how to measure it. So giving people freedom is a terrifying notion for most managers. It's easier to get everyone's butt in their chairs than it is to get everyone clear on what they were hired to *do*.

We also understood that just tossing this definition into a culture doesn't make it change. We knew we needed to paint a picture of what it would look like if the definition of a ROWE were to become a reality. The 13 guideposts we discuss here are that picture—and it's important to note that they are guide*posts*, not guide*lines*. The latter puts people inside the *lines* and tells them exactly what to do or how to act. Guideposts, on the other hand, give people something to aspire to—to move toward. The 13 guideposts are designed to inspire social movement. They're not wishy-washy. If they were, they wouldn't be enticing or interesting or worth discussion. They'd blend in like every other program that touts itself as transformational.

Here are the 13 guideposts and a bit about how they play out:

1. **People at all levels stop doing any activity that is a waste of their time, the customer's time, or the company's money.** This means that people don't spend time in unproductive meetings. They manage communication effectively and respect other people's time. And they eliminate low-priority tasks. It doesn't mean that you skip critical process steps or avoid important client meetings. It also doesn't mean that people can label important work as low priority just to get out of doing it.

2. **Employees have the freedom to work any way they want.** This means autonomy exists at all levels, not just management. People are *where* they need to be *when* they need to be there. The workplace is a tool, not the default location for getting work done. It doesn't mean people *never* come into the physical workplace or that it's okay not to respond to client needs in a timely fashion.

3. **Every day *feels* like Saturday.** This creates the opportunity for everyday integration of work and

personal pursuits without regard to time, place, or schedule—only results. And people are in control of their time every day of the week, not just on weekends. But it doesn't mean no work gets done because everyone is taking the day off or that because I generally do not work on Saturday I don't ever *have* to work but can still collect a paycheck.

4. **People have an unlimited amount of paid time off (PTO) as long as the work gets done.**[1] Work still has to get done with unlimited PTO. This means people focus on results, not tracking time. They manage their energy throughout the year in order to feel rested and energized instead of burned out or overworked. Salaried employees do not need to track time off. This doesn't mean everyone is on permanent paid vacation, that nobody ever gets a vacation, or that people are always calling in sick to avoid doing the work. It doesn't mean people take advantage of others by taking more time off and leaving the work for everyone else.

5. **Work isn't a place you *go;* it's something you *do*.** Everyone works when and where it makes sense. People spend more time focused on the work and less time in rush traffic or other useless time-sucking activities. There is less time "putting in" time, and more time collaborating and communicating to

---

[1]In a ROWE, nonexempt or hourly employees track time/time off in accordance with the US Department of Labor guidelines.

become more effective. And it doesn't mean everyone starts demanding home offices and company-paid mobile phones. It shouldn't lead to a rapid increase in workers' compensation claims or everyone sharing company secrets with competitors. It doesn't mean that *some* work isn't still location-specific.

6. **Arriving at the workplace at 2:00 PM is not considered coming in late. Leaving the workplace at 2:00 PM is not considered leaving early.** Here, the focus is on results, not the clock. And the clock is no indication of work starting or stopping. There is no permission needed to come and go regardless of day or time. But it doesn't mean people fail to put in the time to get work done or that people are slacking. It doesn't mean everyone is out for themselves with no regard for coworkers, clients, or volume of work.

7. **Nobody talks about how many hours they work.** You got it. No more pointless bragging about how early they arrived, how late they stayed, or how they came in on Saturday. Managers focus instead on measurable outcomes and recognize the outcome their employees achieve, not how hard someone appeared to be working or how many hours that person spent in the workplace. It shouldn't lead to the complete breakdown of capacity planning, going against the US Department of Labor guidelines, or milking the system to put in as little time/effort as possible.

8. *Every* **meeting is optional.** This guidepost gives managers the most anxiety, which is one reason why we dedicate a whole chapter of this book just to meetings. It's necessary to make each employee stop and question the time spent in meetings (after all, it equals money!) and make better decisions about whether a particular meeting is necessary or the best way to drive results. (Our clients tell us 30 to 80 percent of time spent in meetings is unproductive or wasted.) You can substantially diminish the time that employees spend in unproductive meetings. And people who opt-in to a meeting are fully present and undistracted by other priorities. Recurring meetings are greatly reduced, and people make decisions faster. It does not mean people decline all meetings or those that drive outcomes. It doesn't mean people become disrespectful of client or coworker needs or make decisions they can't be trusted to make.

9. **It's okay to grocery shop on a Wednesday morning, catch a movie on a Tuesday afternoon, or take a nap on a Thursday afternoon.** In a ROWE, people are getting more of what's important done in *all* aspects of their lives. And managers are setting clear and measurable goals on a continual basis, not as an annual or biannual event. Natural cross-training and an "I've got your back" team mentality develops, compelling the group to team up on client needs in a seamless fashion. As a result, client satisfaction goes up. It certainly doesn't mean people ignore the business to have fun or that a

company fails to respond to client needs. And an entitlement attitude doesn't all of a sudden rear its ugly head. It doesn't mean that if I have a critical event at 2 PM on Tuesday that I blow it off to go to the matinee.

10. **There are no work schedules.** Flexibility does not need to be managed; it manages itself. Working hours are expanding, not hours worked. And employees and teams make good decisions about how they spend their time and are meeting business needs in a fluid manner. Managers do not dictate schedules or core hours. It doesn't mean everyone decides to work from 5 PM to 11 PM or that complete chaos ensues—and it doesn't create the complete breakdown of business process and continuity. It doesn't mean that if a retail store opens at 10:00 AM, nobody is there to open the doors.

11. **Nobody feels guilty, overworked, or stressed out.** This is important! People are taking care of their own and the business' needs, which means that they feel better about *everything*. They're motivated by working in an environment of trust and openness versus fear and control. People take better care of their health and well-being; they get more rest, which allows them to think clearly and make better decisions in all areas of their lives. It doesn't mean people become apathetic or unmotivated or start working less to reduce stress.

12. **There aren't any last-minute fire drills.** This promotes a culture that is proactive instead of

reactive. Fire drills are simply the result of poor planning. There's no more crying wolf; your organization won't measure importance based on avoidable heroic efforts. Planning becomes the *norm* (imagine that!). It doesn't mean that business emergencies never happen or that the workforce becomes static—or that people make decisions without appropriate buy-in or available resources.

13. **There is *no judgment* about how you spend your time.** Time is a negotiable, nonrenewable commodity, which prompts a greater level of respect to grow, both for the work *and* the people who do it. The workplace becomes focused on the bottom line. Showing up is about the work, not a place. It doesn't mean people suddenly start disrespecting management or that a total breakdown of company values or confusion and lack of purpose emerges.

We stand by the new definition of *work* and the 13 guideposts. And since we left Best Buy in 2007, we've worked with many organizations across multiple industries and disciplines to facilitate adoption of a ROWE using this platform. We still hear daily protests that people in countless occupations can't change to a ROWE: receptionists, surgeons, zookeepers, bus drivers, retail workers, or nurses, just to name a few.

Really?

You don't want surgeons, retail workers, and receptionists to focus on *RESULTS?* This is the major difference between a ROWE and an environment that embraces "flexibility." A ROWE focuses on ensuring that each and every person is absolutely clear about what they were hired to do—and then making sure they do it. Flexibility, on the other hand, is all about playing games with schedules. In a ROWE, everyone is treated like an adult. They don't ask permission to leave early, because they are accountable to the work. In a ROWE, no results equals no job. You'll see what we mean as you dive into the book. We'll give you concrete examples of how this works—and the role of a manager in driving this type of culture—throughout.

With flexibility, the manager acts as a parent who doles out accommodations to the chosen few, which, in turn, creates a hostile workforce where guilt, complacency, stress, resentment, disrespect, and low morale all thrive.

You would think organizations would be jumping on the bandwagon, raising their hands and yelling, "Me next, me next!" to create a culture where productivity sky-rockets, talent sticks, individual and team capacity expands, wasted time is annihilated, results and measures become crystal clear, and managers develop into coaches and mentors who manage performance on a daily basis. *You would think*. But here's what we learned over the past nine years:

We've talked to leaders and organizations throughout North America, South America, Europe, Australia, and Asia and found that, all over the globe, people are *attracted* to the idea. They are craving real, foundational change and see a ROWE as a possibility for it. And then they try to make it happen in a DIY fashion. This is good.

After all, a ROWE in its essence is social change. It's not top-down. It's a bottom-up process and needs to be owned by everyone. It requires that people abandon certain deeply held beliefs:

- You need face-to-face communication to build effective relationships.
- People who are at work are working.
- Communication is more effective when everyone is in the office.
- You have to come in early and stay late to get ahead.
- If someone leaves early, that person has stopped working.
- Office hours are important to the customer.

It's hard to let go of these.

And we've learned people want to "do ROWE" a little at a time. They want to take pieces of the process, bits of the idea, and dabble in making small changes. They want to hold on to some level of control and are hesitant to go all the way. They want to change the wording in the guideposts (caution: changing the wording is a sneaky way to keep the status quo intact). They have some understandable worries: What if all my people stop working? How will I be able to tell if people are working? How will I know when people are available? What about vacation?

Most big corporations don't want us to come in and mess up their culture. If it's going to get messed up, they want to do it on their own—not have some half-crazed consultant come in and grant freedom to people they believe can't handle it. They want to own the process, learn how to do it, and install it themselves. That way it becomes theirs. This is also good—because *owning* a social change is what makes it happen.

Cali and I have had nightmares over this DIY mentality. We know how difficult culture change is, and we want a ROWE to remain pure and intact. If you say you're in a ROWE, we want it to *really be* a ROWE—or at least honestly moving toward making the guideposts come to life. It's not okay to institute a watered-down "We're flexible here" version of a ROWE. "We're a ROWE! We let our people leave early sometimes!" is *not* a ROWE. We've made it our goal to make ROWE the status quo and differentiate it from all other flavor-of-the-month corporate team-building programs. We've developed an efficient and effective process to reshape the culture. It's disruptive social change. We figured it out and now know what works. It's been tough to relinquish the control we want to have, but it's a lesson well learned.

We are happy to report that our company, CultureRx, has successfully worked with organizations to implement a ROWE through hands-on training. We've worked with government, child care, manufacturing, education, nonprofit foundations, large and small businesses, and union shops with both exempt and nonexempt employees. We've trained teams and companies with department functions that include call centers, finance/accounting, advertising, marketing, investment services, sales, IT/network infrastructure, human resources, project management, vendor management, retail operations,

Web design, communications, child care, direct care, insurance agencies, a crime lab, and legal.

Most important, we've learned a lot from these implementations that we will pass along in more detail in this book. From government, for example—local, state, and federal—we learned how pervasive the taxpayer expectation is that government workers put in their hours in an office. After all, that's what our taxpayer dollars are paying for, right? This is a hard perception to break. We're not really paying for people to "put in time"; we're paying for our governments to produce results.

We learned from the child care industry that checklists are for checking things off but not always actually doing what's required. "I checked off the checklist . . . check!" However, if they don't have a checklist, child care providers actually *pay attention* to what's best for the child. They accomplish whatever is on the checklist naturally by putting the child's needs first.

In education, we learned that it's not only instructors who need to be able to make commonsense decisions about how to get to their results, but students, too. We realized that there's unfortunately a great deal of rhetoric in the education arena about catering to students' unique needs but that "the way we've always done things" tends to win out.

We readily recognize that organizations and teams will continue to require assistance, support, nudging, and tools as they evolve their work cultures.

As such, this book will share our real-world experiences in training these organizations to become an authenic ROWE. And we'll really get into the weeds. We'll give you tried-and-true tips and tricks that managers have used to evolve their work*place* into a results-only work*force*. We've incorporated what we've learned over the past 9 years. We've transformed the process, given it more prescriptive elements to help the change evolve, and set it free.

A ROWE doesn't need to be managed. It needs to be accessible, approachable, and nonthreatening. And we've made peace with the fact that it can be a little messy at times.

So think of this as your field guide to the future of work and your evolution as a manager.

You'll notice that this book is a conversation between Cali and me along with feedback from some ROWE companies. The development of a ROWE has been a series of ongoing conversations, experimentation, refinement, and ultimately, success. We've laughed, we've cried, and we've cheered. We've watched the unimaginable happen. We've seen people take back their lives and have seen businesses thrive. We've experienced and helped others experience what people tell us they once considered an unobtainable utopia. Each person living the life he or she wants to live on his or her own terms could be described as utopia, couldn't it? And it's *achievable*. In so many places, across all kinds of businesses, it *has* been achieved. Take this example from Eric Severson, senior vice president of talent at Gap North America, a leading global specialty retailer:

> Every division that has adopted ROWE has seen significantly improved operating and financial performance since we've used the CultureRx proven process to implement it. It started with Gap Outlet,

which had its highest sales and earnings performance ever post-ROWE and continues to overachieve. Then Gap brand—which has been in a slump for most of 10 years—had the best performance in a decade during the first 6 months of the 2012 fiscal year (post-2011 ROWE implementation). Gap Inc. Direct (online, Athleta, and Piperlime) already had nearly a decade of nonstop breakthrough performance, which has continued after their ROWE implementation. Finally, Banana Republic has also experienced the best business in the past year—post-ROWE migration—than it has seen in at least 5 years. Old Navy has now committed to implementing ROWE. Today, based on the strength of all of our North America businesses (all of which are ROWEs except Old Navy), we reached a 12-year-high stock price of $35.99. While I would never try to argue that ROWE is singularly responsible for this performance, there is no doubt in my mind that it is a significant contributing factor.

In the end, the one thing that has remained constant is our dedication to the dream and each other. This book is our extension of that conversation. Sometimes you'll see Cali taking the reins and sometimes me. But in the end, our goal is the same: to make ROWEs the status quo and abolish management-controlled flexibility once and for all.

If you think a ROWE is just another passing fancy, think again.

—**Jody Thompson**

1

Wake Up!

Go Beyond Telework

Nothing like starting out a book with a command, right? Consider it fair warning, though; this is a taste of the way we're going to interact with you as you continue reading. We're not going to pussyfoot around and make you wonder what we're *really* trying to say. You're going to know exactly how to move into the twenty-first century as a manager who is focused on what matters.

Now, could it get any more daunting to think about how things need to change as we continue down the road of this century? We talk with CEO after CEO who says "What got us to this point of success over the past

50 years will not keep us successful over the *next* 50 but we don't have a map that tells us what to change or how to do it." That's one of the reasons we decided to write this book, and I must admit that although I was excited to write it, I was also pretty anxious. Distilling the messages we want to share for approaching work and management for the next 87 years of this century (and maybe beyond) isn't something you can just sit down and whip out. But then I remembered something. When Jody and I were creating the Results-Only Work Environment (ROWE)—and experimenting with ways to design a work environment that catalyzed maximum happiness and productivity for employees' lives—we realized something. And that something *literally* made us stop in our tracks. I can vividly recall both of us walking back to our cubicles (ah, yes, the lovely cubicles) from Sandy's Place (Best Buy's in-house cafeteria), stopping at the same time, and saying, "Wait a minute. What we're doing is *simplifying* things. One of the reasons people are grabbing onto this is because we're taking away, not adding. We're not laying a program on top of an already screwed-up culture. We're rewiring the screwed-up culture so that anything that is added in the future will actually *work*." We weren't adding to the fog that hung over everyone's heads. We were helping people clear that away so that they could see, *really* see, how the world could be different.

As we started implementing a ROWE at Best Buy one department at a time, we could spot the differences in those groups immediately. And it wasn't just in their business results; it was in their attitudes, the way they

communicated with one another, the way they confidently held themselves as they walked through the main
hub area of the campus, and the way their eyes lit up
when we talked with them.

Then we'd walk by the corporate cafeteria at Best
Buy, see people who had not transitioned to a ROWE
yet, and say to each other, "Look at all of them in there.
They're still sleeping." By *sleeping*, we meant that they
hadn't been awakened yet to this world, one where
they were free to make their own decisions, own their
own time, feel attached to the ultimate outcome, and
contribute to the organization and society the way they
really *wanted to*. Those who hadn't gone to a ROWE yet
still had empty eyes that were glazed over; they had
resigned themselves to waiting for retirement to catch
some glimpses of happiness. They hadn't had that fire lit
from inside yet. They were still walking around like they
were trying to claw their way out of the world that was
holding them back from *living*.

Part of this state of sleeping is not even being aware
of what you're missing. If you've never experienced what
it's like to just do what you need to according to what *makes
sense* instead of what time or day of the week it is, then
you're sleeping. If you know it would be better to grocery
shop on a Tuesday morning when it would take you 30
minutes instead of going on Sunday when it will take you
2 hours but you go on Sunday anyway, you're sleeping.
If you keep telling your kids *every* day, "I can't have
breakfast with you because I have to be at work by 8 AM,"
you're sleeping. If you've been putting off your hobbies,
the things you love to do, and the people you love

and saving opportunities for retirement, you're sleeping. Like we said in *Why Work Sucks and How to Fix It*, we're programmed to think work is supposed to be awful. And sometimes, just *sometimes*, there might be glimmers of hope.

Case in point: One of the statements we use in a previous version of our pre-implementation survey to measure a work culture's baseline perception before teams go through ROWE training is, "I have complete control over how I spend my time every day." Employees use a Likert scale of Strongly Disagree, Disagree, Neither Agree nor Disagree, Agree, or Strongly Agree to rate the statements. For some clients, the response to this statement was fairly high, with most employees in the Agree and Strongly Agree categories.

Another survey entry stated: "I could arrive to the office at 11 AM or leave at 2 PM on any given day, not be judged, and not feel guilty." For the same clients where employees agreed or strongly agreed they had complete control over how they spent their time every day, this statement would come back with employees disagreeing or strongly disagreeing.

What does this tell us? People *want* to feel like they have autonomy. They want to be able to feel good about the amount of control they have over their lives and how they use their time. No one wants to truly admit feeling like a puppet whose life has been run by someone else or to face 1,023 deathbed regrets that all result from being unable to really enjoy his or her time on Earth. So people respond to the first statement the way they *want* to think things are. But when it really comes down to it, it's not real. This is where the second statement comes in. When employees are forced to admit if they're actually executing on the control they *think* they have, they're not—plain and simple.

Jody: I remember hearing from a number of people that they were "ruined" after reading *Why Work Sucks and How to Fix It*, because it had opened their eyes to what was really missing; all the little perks they were "allowed" to have seemed empty. Now, all of a sudden—rather than being eternally grateful for being allowed to leave early on a Friday—they realized how absurd their world was. They became angered by how little control they had and realized it wasn't going to get any better. They knew that they could no longer be complacent and pretend everything was as good as it was ever going to get. Bottom line? It was unacceptable.

Enter managers.

The twenty-first century is about you waking up. And we wrote this book because we have faith that managers can do that.

We can already hear some of you saying, "Things are going so well with my business (or in my team). Good thing I'm already awake!" You might as well be saying, "Come and get me, competition. I've given it all I've got!" Really? We're actually surprised sometimes by how many leaders say, "Well, we don't really need to move to a ROWE right now. Maybe next year." Maybe next year we can get our heads out of the sand and make sure we're results-focused. Another year of focusing on the wrong things won't hurt. Why not? We've been doing it for 40, 50, 60, or more years already.

WAKE UP.

You with us?

Good. (And if not, Jody will probably kick your ass.)

On your way to fully waking up in the twenty-first century and helping others do so as well, it's time to start using the word *work* as a verb instead of a noun. As we discussed in *Why Work Sucks and How to Fix It*, work is *something we do*, not a place we go. Now we need to take those pretty words a bit further.

Every time we say, "I'm going to work now," that promotes work as a place.

Every time we say, "I'm not at work yet," that relays, "My brain is off."

Every time we ask someone, "When are you getting to work?" we're basically saying, "The physical location *is* work."

When engaging with a group of nurses at a direct health care setting awhile back, we asked them what the most impactful part of a ROWE was for them. They agreed that it was coming to this incredibly crucial realization: that work wasn't a place they went; it was something they did. This was powerful for me and, I have to admit, somewhat unexpected. Even for this group of people—who have residents to care for in specific locations—*work* had turned into a verb. They admitted that they thought about work even when they weren't in the care facilities, not because anyone was forcing them to, but because that's the way our brains work. One nurse said, "I might be at home cooking dinner, and I start feeling anxious about how Miss Betty is doing. I'll call one of the nurses on shift to tell her that Miss Betty mentioned she might want to listen to some music tonight before going to sleep." This is a perfect example of how the nurses didn't have to *go* to work to *do* work. None of us do. If you're a zookeeper, the animals you care for are obviously at the zoo. But this doesn't mean you don't think about them and have ideas about how to care for them while you're not at the zoo. If you're a bus driver, you don't need to be on the bus to think about how tomorrow, when Ted gets on at 32nd and Smith Street, you're going to ask how his father is doing now that he's living in Arizona.

As *work* continues to shift from a noun to a verb, there's another remnant of the twentieth century that we can burn at the stake: the terms *remote work*, *virtual work*, and *mobile work*. Work is *work*—period.

Remote work insinuates that we're away from something, a physical location where work *should* be done. And really, isn't *all* work mobile? We always have our brains with us and could be thinking about work at any given moment. If I'm a retail employee taking a shower, I might think about a customer interaction I had that day and how I could improve the next. Am I working? Am I "mobile"? Maybe I'm a doctor imagining a new way to engage my pediatric patients while I'm falling asleep at night. Whether we're described as knowledge workers or not, our brains simply never turn off. And *virtual work* . . . as opposed to what? *Real* work? Enough of these terms. We're simplifying things, remember?

Along with this simplification, we can also stop calling people names. That's right—labeling people is so 1990. Words to remove from your vocabulary if you're serious about moving into the twenty-first century include the following: *flex worker, teleworker, remote worker, virtual worker, mobile worker, telecommuter* . . . and, if we had it our way, *part-* and *full-timer*. Since when do we need to stick labels on people to be able to refer to them? Why do we label people in the first place? Simple: to mark that they are doing something different from the norm. And the insinuation that comes with the labeling is that they are doing something different from what they're *supposed* to be doing. "This is Jim. He's one of our remote workers." How about "This is Jim. He does great work for us!" Try it. It's one more step in the simplification process that will make you, and your employees, feel less constrained and contained by the practices of last century.

Okay, here comes a big one. Prepare yourself for the removal of a word that's been thrown around for the past 40 years but has done *nothing* to get us closer to focusing on results:

Flexibility—the new "F" word.

If you're cheering, you're with us. If your brow is furrowed, you're not quite sure why flexibility is so bad. If you're fuming, it's because you think flexibility has come a long way and you think we're disrespecting that. We've heard it all, and we're prepared to explain.

Flexibility had a place past century as a way to give employees some breathing room in their hectic, chaotic lives. Coming in later, leaving early, working shorter days, working longer days with Fridays off—there were any number of "flexible work options" that organizations might offer to employees. And managers (well, most of them) have always wanted to motivate employees to do their best work. But they're surrounded by employees buzzing about how they want work/life balance, complaining that they're stressed out, and threatening to leave if something doesn't change. Employees commiserate with one another daily about how they wish managers understood that they have lives in addition to the job. So to make it all stop and give them what they want, many managers instituted some flexibility. Employees were usually (and understandably) excited about this. They started chatting with one another about how their managers were so understanding, instead of venting about how much they sucked because they didn't understand how many responsibilities they have in their lives. Managers felt like superheroes for a moment, because they were able to swoop in and give people what they needed.

But as fast as that moment arrived, it's now gone. What managers thought would be the magic move to end all the madness creates even *more* chaos than they had started with. Everyone is focused on working from home for 4 days a week, and now they're fighting about it. Half the team spends a good portion of the day complaining about how it's not fair that some people get to come in at 8:30 AM instead of 8:00 AM. It seems like a good idea at this point to establish some guidelines around the flexibility, to make sure that employees know what the core hours are, who can be flexible and who can't, and what the process is for requesting different schedules.

Jody: I'm sometimes disheartened when talking to our human resources (HR) partners in client organizations and I hear about how much time and energy they put into creating policies for work that doesn't take place in the office. Just recently, I had a conversation about some *crazed employees* who wanted to work from a location other than the office 100 percent of the time—when they came into the office every day prior to being in a ROWE. HR was busily trying to write policy around this. Perhaps we should tell them they have to be in the office at least 2 days a month! Our low performers shouldn't have this privilege! What bumpers can we put in place to discourage this behavior? WHAT? *Everyone* was hired to do a job. They need to be clear about their measurable results. If they can't meet results, no job. HR should be coaching managers to be results-focused and objective, and not to cling to old subjective beliefs about what work should look and feel like. This department is in a unique position to stop the insanity—and it's a role they must embrace.

What began as a move on the manager's part to alleviate stress levels and assist employees with their everyday lives has now turned into a different kind of stress—all of which sits on managers' shoulders. They're stuck in a world of managing flexibility (say that aloud and notice how crazy it sounds—"managing" something that's supposed to be "flexible"?). They're in charge of how it happens, when it happens, where it happens, and who gets it. And not necessarily because it's what they *want* to be doing, but if no one takes control of it, how will the work ever get done?

Flexibility *is* the new "F" word.

It's disguised itself long enough as something that will help employees and be the "perk" that will catalyze more productivity, higher engagement levels, and overall happiness (in other words, it will stop employees from complaining about their lack of work/life balance). But flexibility is a trap. Like a shiny object, it takes everyone's eye off the ball: the results that employees need to achieve for organizations to thrive. Experts will try to tell you that you can have both: be focused on the work and also encourage people to work in a flexible manner. They might have you name it something different like Work-flex, but don't be fooled. They'll even tell you that flexibility is a business imperative that you must infuse into your culture to get the most out of your people. But that's not the way it works. You're either focused on results *or* flexibility.

It's really quite simple: When flexibility is in the mix, that's what people think about first. Results come second. They approach it as, "This is the way I want to work. Now let's hope I can get everything done this way."

When you're focused on results, however, flexibility manages itself. Employees are always looking at results *first* and then figuring out how to accomplish them. In these situations, they say, "Here's what I have to achieve. What's the best way to do that?"

Once the word *flexibility* enters the equation, it simply becomes another thing to manage. Remember what we're doing in this chapter: simplifying. Leave *flexibility* out of your vocabulary and see how accountability and productivity rise. Just the act of removing the word *flexibility* from your language or redirecting the conversation can be difficult to think about, so here are some quick, easy ways to start.

During the Recruiting Process

Candidate: Do you offer flexibility?

Recruiter/hiring manager: We focus on results here. How you work, where you work, and when you work is completely up to you.

Candidate: But how much flexibility do you permit?

Recruiter/hiring manager: We don't manage it. It's completely up to you to make good, smart decisions about how to achieve your results.

Candidate: So do you have flexible work schedules or . . . ?

Recruiter/hiring manager: No. We trust our employees to manage their time how they best see fit. Anything goes as long as you meet your results.

With a Current Employee

Employee: I'd like to request some flexibility.

Manager: Let's talk about the results you're expected to achieve. From there, it's up to you to figure out how you'll make that happen.

Employee: But I want a fair amount of flexibility. I'm going back to school next quarter.

Manager: I'm here to manage results, not how you reach them. Let's make sure we're on the same page with what you need to achieve.

Employee: I'd like the comfort of knowing I'll be able to go back to school, so will we be able to work out my schedule?

Manager: Based on the results you need to achieve, you'll work out however you can do that and go back to school. Let's chat about those and how we're measuring them to make sure we're on the same page.

With a Peer

Peer: I'm thinking we should increase our level of flexibility to try to improve our engagement scores.

You: Let's focus on making sure everyone is clear about what they need to deliver and how they'll be measured. I think that's key to engagement.

Peer: But you've heard people begging to be able to work remotely. Let's try to figure out something that will work.

You: Whether people are working remotely or in the office, we still need to be sure they're focused on the right things. We need to start there.

With a Manager

Your manager: I've noticed you've been coming and going at some odd times over the past few weeks. If you're needing some more flexibility, we can talk about some options for your schedule.

You: I've actually found that I'm better able to focus on my results and serve my customers when I make those smart decisions every day about how I approach the work.

Your manager: Well, even though we don't have any real formal flexibility options, I think we can work something out.

You: Have you noticed anything slipping with my performance or my customers over the past few weeks?

Your manager: No, not at all.

You: Well, then I think we should just keep focusing on that and not worry about placing me into a flexibility box. If something suffers with my performance, let's talk about *that*.

With a Client/Customer

Client: I came by to see you yesterday, and you weren't around. That's actually happened the past couple of times I've dropped by. What's your schedule these days?

You: We didn't have an appointment that I missed, did we?

Client: No, no—nothing like that. Just swung in and didn't find you here.

You: I definitely want to make sure you get what you need when you need it. Call or e-mail me anytime, and I'm more than happy to set up a face-to-face appointment. I want to be sure you receive superior service from us.

Client: Well, if you tell me your schedule, then I'll just
know when to stop by.
You: I work according to my clients' needs, so every day
looks different. Is there something you need?

Kyle Pederson, owner of Learner's Edge—a client
of ours that offers leading-edge, thought-provoking,
versatile graduate credit courses for teachers—sums it
up well:

> ROWE is simply a more respectful, adult way of
> doing business. It's more respectful because it
> [entails] treating adults as adults. Who has given me,
> as a manager, the right to control the lives of my
> employees to such a degree as is typical in traditional
> work environments? In the traditional scenario, I
> dictate a number of things: how many weeks/hours
> of paid time off an employee gets; whether being
> 15–20 minutes late for a scheduled shift should be
> marked on a time card; whether a long lunch should
> result in an extended closing time; whether caring
> for a sick child is a good enough reason for not
> coming in, etc. The list is endless. And even in
> flexible work environments, where the specific
> examples of the heavy hand of management might
> be less onerous, the same management power
> exists—just beneath the surface.

In the end, you want everyone in your organization
to go from thinking, "I need some flexibility," to "I own
the work, and it's up to *me* to decide how I'm going to get

it done."And you can bet word will spread that yours is the organization to work for when the employee mind-set changes like this. Stopping the flexibility game and focusing on results will set you on a whole new platform for attracting and retaining talent. John Thompson, executive vice president of Dot Com at Best Buy, may have said it best when he stated, "All things being equal—great company, great business performance, great pay grades, great opportunities to grow and develop—with all things being equal, ROWE can, and will be, the swing factor."

Right now, candidates go from organization to organization hearing the same tired spiels. Here's what we offer, here's how things work, here's how much vacation time you'll get, here's your cube. How motivating. Now, try this on for size:

The "We're Flexible Work Environment"	A Results-Only Work Environment
I get 3 weeks of vacation/year.	I manage my time all of the time.
I get 6 sick days/year.	I own the outcome of my work.
No merit increases this year.	Thank you for my freedom.
I get 12 weeks to bond with my new baby.	I *feel* like I'm always on maternity leave.
We have a fitness center!	I go to the gym in my neighborhood.
I can't wait to retire.	I *feel* like I'm already retired.

One of the contemporary benefits that's been catching on more and more in organizations is the idea of unlimited vacation. We predict that a growing number of organizations will try jumping into this realm as this century continues. After all, about 57 percent of working Americans ended 2011 with an average of 11 unused vacation days, according to a Harris Interactive study. Although the intent behind instituting unlimited vacation is good, there are three main issues that may arise as you try to move in this direction:

1. Employees have been building up their vacation balances so that they get the paid value when they leave the organization. Instituting unlimited vacation and stopping the accrual practice as people have known it for decades might feel like you're closing down one of their savings accounts.

2. Employees with seniority might be upset that those just entering the organization will have the same amount of vacation time they do.

3. Sometimes people won't even know what unlimited vacation means. They'll interpret it as "no more vacation."

So how do you head these off? Our risk mitigation strategy of choice is to implement a ROWE *before* instituting unlimited paid time off. It will be a smoother transition—believe us. It's basically a choice of whether you want to have 70 percent of your population kicking and screaming as you drag them along or if you want to have somewhat of an easier time by reducing that cranky group to just 30 percent. Not everyone will be happy with the change, but when *is* everyone happy at the same time?

This at least allows you to increase the amount of happy campers by as much as possible.

Why the increase of people cheering about unlimited paid time off when a ROWE is already instituted? To remove a piece of work culture as strong as vacation time—and have (most) employees welcome and accept that removal—they need to let go on their terms. It can't be something the organization forces on them from out of the blue that requires them to undergo the grief cycle. Here's how it happens:

Learner's Edge executive director Julie Yaeger shares how her company's on-site ROWE training and subsequent evolution set the foundation for moving into a state of unlimited paid time off naturally instead of abruptly:

> As a company, we did not bank vacation days; so when we began ROWE in October of 2011, we encouraged employees to use their vacation days through December—as we had done each year. It became clear to us during the first 3 months of ROWE, as employees were following the process of meeting responsibilities while not feeling tied to the office, that "giving" personal or vacation days just didn't seem to make sense. Our employees [took accountability for owning] their time, as we wanted—and we found that there was quite a natural transition from "giving" a number of days to be taken to simply having unlimited days. We did wait until the customary contractual and calendar break, so all employees had a chance to "use up" what days

had been given; and would recommend that process to others that don't bank, so no one felt they "lost" anything.

Another question is probably crossing your minds as we're talking about the future. What about all of this for nonexempt (hourly) employees? Can *they* have unlimited vacation? What about the regulations that exist that refer to tracking time? The US Department of Labor does require nonexempt employees to track the hours they work, which can seem very contradictory to focusing on results and letting that focus drive success. As you might imagine, we'd like to bring the Department of Labor and the powers-that-be who are keeping these regulations alive into the twenty-first century, too. We're working on it, but it hasn't happened yet. So, in the meantime, ROWE organizations have identified how to comply with these regulations but also help nonexempt employees move as close as they can to focusing on what's important: results, not time. ROWE organizations solve this problem by instituting what some call auto pay. In this system, nonexempt employees in the private sector are paid for 40 hours per week, regardless of whether they work fewer hours. According to Department of Labor regulations, nonexempt employees must track the time they work and record it according to company compliance policies. The key with auto pay is that if employees work fewer than 40 hours in a week, they are still paid for 40. If they work more than 40 hours, they are paid overtime, consistent with Department of Labor regulations.

Just like exempt employees, nonexempt employees become more efficient in a ROWE. But it doesn't take long for nonexempt employees to realize that they won't get paid their "full" paycheck if they work fewer than 40 hours. Efficiency is punished in the twentieth-century system, so most nonexempt employees have learned to spread out their work to get their 40 hours of pay. If you want to reward efficiency, auto pay is an important move to make. Jodie Monson is a business partner for corporate planning and functions at our client H.B. Fuller, a leading global adhesives manufacturer and solution provider. After completing our on-site training, Monson stated,

> The focus on results, planning, and the ultimate in work/life balance were the key concepts that drew us to ROWE like bears to honey. At H.B. Fuller, we were committed to enhancing employee engagement. We spoke about empowering employees, building a high-performance culture, and retaining our top talent. Implementing a Results-Only Work Environment with CultureRx was an opportunity to walk the talk we'd been hearing from executive leadership.

> Once we made the decision to transition to a ROWE, we needed the same latitude extended to salaried and nonexempt employees. We'd fall short on demonstrating a shift from time-focused to results-focused if we continued to measure our nonexempt employees by the number of hours they worked.

Unfortunately, federal, state, and local laws that were originally established to protect nonexempt employees require that this pool of workers record their hours on a weekly basis. Our first inclination was to pay everyone based on a fixed salary; however, we quickly learned from our legal staff that this wasn't a feasible legal solution on job classifications—since certain classifications required overtime pay for more than 40 hours worked in a week. Therefore, these same roles required time tracking.

We therefore established a policy that nonexempt employees would be paid for at least 40 hours per week, regardless of how many hours they worked, as long as they were meeting their expected results. We set up our time tracking system with a ROWE code that was to be used at the end of the pay period to get the recorded hours to 40 if needed. Overtime would still be paid for hours in excess of 40.

I know what you're thinking; does anyone use the ROWE code? The answer is YES. Employees have clearly set expectations, and in most cases, detailed service-level agreements. If they are meeting their expectations, delivering results, and doing it in fewer than 40 hours for the week, it is a win for everyone! H.B. Fuller is a pay-for-performance company [that focuses] on results. We are walking the talk. Employees are embracing the ability to deliver results to H.B. Fuller while being empowered to manage their lives.

Another outdated time element that is still very much alive in work culture is the concept of billable hours. I don't mean outdated as in organizations aren't doing this anymore (because they are); I mean outdated as in old, not necessary, and doesn't fit into where the world of work is going. Once you're in the ROWE mind-set, the notion of billable hours turns into a hot potato; you want to get rid of it right away and sure as hell don't want to be the last one in your industry holding onto it. It becomes so ludicrous to even think about charging clients for *time* that you want to determine another solution immediately. This is what happened at Diaz & Cooper, a Miami-based Web development and digital marketing agency.

When Diaz & Cooper signed on for our on-site ROWE training, management had already been kicking around the idea that hourly billing and time sheets were counterproductive, not to mention that the hourly billing model was ineffective and self-limiting. "Worse yet," said agency president Otmara "Omi" Diaz-Cooper, "billing by the hour reduces the work we do to a commodity." Continuing to bow to time will keep producing these scenarios, shared by Diaz-Cooper:

- John gritted his teeth as he tried to recall how many hours he'd spent on the e-mail project; "I'll just put in 3 hours; yeah, that sounds about right." He'd fallen behind on his time sheets for the week and now was scrambling to get them done before his boss questioned him . . . again.
- Barbara sat idly as she often did at the end of the month. She was supposed to be processing invoices,

but because many employees had not turned in their time sheets, she couldn't do a darned thing—except sit at her desk and try to look busy. She worried that her boss would be mad that the billing cycle would be delayed . . . again.

- Charlie looked at the layout and sighed. He knew he could do a lot better with the colors and copy placement if only he had a few more hours to work on the piece. But he checked his task list and all of the design hours on the project were already used up, so he just gave up on it being an award winner . . . again.

"These scenarios pass for normal daily working conditions in almost every ad agency in the world. The culture of estimating, keeping track of, billing by time and worrying about not having enough *time* to count the time is so prevalent that it's practically a religion," Diaz-Cooper states.

She goes on to explain, "As value pricing aligns your financial interests with those of your clients, so does ROWE align your values with those of your workforce."

Speaking of aligning values with those of your workforce, another topic that we must address here is health and wellness programs in organizations. As we discuss the future of the work world—and having you waking up, little by little—it's time to recognize that these programs aren't the means to the end you're looking for. It always strikes us as very odd that the same organizations that chain their employees to their cubes from 8:00 to 5:00 Monday through Friday are the same ones that invest thousands, sometimes millions, of dollars on programs that are meant to improve employee well-being. In fact, before we created ROWE, I was intimately connected to the health and wellness programs at Best Buy. When the organization built their state-of-the-art 16,000-square-foot fitness and wellness center, I was heading up a committee that was supposed to figure out how to increase employee utilization of the facility. The problem the organization was trying to solve? The center was packed before 8:00 AM, at lunchtime, and after 5:00 PM. During the other times of day, it was a ghost town. In *my* head, the reason for that was clear. And perhaps that was because I was entrenched in the everyday employee conversations that shed light on the answer: "If I'm seen in the fitness center and not at my desk at 10:00 AM, there will be hell to pay." The belief permeating the culture was that people who used the fitness center at those "unacceptable" times were slackers. But my thoughts about this fell on painfully deaf ears. Instead, leadership wanted to schedule communications to come from them about their support for employee utilization of the fitness center in conjunction with the organization's goals for improving employee well-being and bringing down health claims costs. Gag me. No amount of communication was going to make employees think they were safe from the wrath of Sludge, the language in the work environment that judges how people spend their time. Examples of Sludge:

"Wow, did you see Joe in the fitness center at 2:00 PM? Wish I had time to run on the treadmill like that!"

"I saw Lisa signed up for the 1:00 PM yoga class. Isn't she working on that big project? Guess we know where *her* priorities are."

Jody: It certainly didn't bode well for my *mental* health and well-being to be huffing and puffing away on the treadmill—in my spandex—when my boss walked by. Do I want my boss or coworkers to see me red, puffy, and sweating? I definitely don't want to admit I'm out of shape but I *really* don't want to display that in a place where the person who controls the fate of my promotion might see me. Worse yet, here I am with headphones on trying to be anonymous, and a coworker jumps on the treadmill next to me to ask me about a project! Are you kidding me? My physical health and well-being may have been improving, but mentally, I was a step away from institutionalization. And don't even get me started on the shower room . . ."

The solution to this challenge of how to improve employee health and wellness seems so clear. Yet organizations position themselves as far away from it as they can get. Heaven forbid we actually lower blood pressure, improve mental health, combat obesity, and help people exercise more frequently by *giving them control* over their time and lives! In the December 2011 *Journal of Health and Social Behavior*, a study by University of Minnesota professors Phyllis Moen and Erin Kelly discussed changes in the health behaviors and actual health of employees who had undergone ROWE training. They then measured those changes against those who hadn't completed training. The data show that a ROWE isn't just a morale booster; it's a way to improve your workforce's health and productivity. Professor Phyllis Moen shares, "These results show that working conditions—not just personal situations—can actually help make people healthy or unhealthy."

The following were associated with employees who reported better health behaviors in the study:

✓ More sleep (almost an extra hour each night)
✓ More exercise
✓ Ability to stay home when sick
✓ Early treatment for illness

Employees also reported greater schedule control and less work/family conflict, which led to greater health and well-being:

✓ Improved mental well-being
✓ Reduced stress
✓ Greater feelings of being in control of one's life
✓ Better overall health
✓ Improved energy

Another 2011 study showed that employees lowered their turnover intentions and actually turned over less than employees not in a ROWE. "There's definitely a business case for improving employee health and well-being by giving people control over how they spend their time—which is exactly what ROWE does," says Erin Kelly, professor of sociology at the University of Minnesota. "It's important for organizations to understand that these initiatives have more to do with the level of autonomy they give employees than with the latest fad program."

One of the most important things to recognize about where we're at with "work" is that people are *done* with flavor-of-the-month programs. You've used up your free chances to try things and then take them away or to try things because they sound good but aren't supported by leadership. Employees are completely numb to anything new that comes in. They don't want to get attached, because they are all too aware of what will happen next. So why waste the energy trying to support Mr. or Ms. Big Cheese's latest whim?

The future is not about the disingenuous pacification of employees. The employees of the twenty-first century can see right through that. The future is about stripping away all the layers of "management" skin that have formed over the past century and actually living within your own skin. It's about doing what's right and rejecting the management "devil on the shoulder" voice that says, "But that's not what a good manager does."

The *good manager* has died. *You* have been awakened.

Typical Questions

The following are typical questions managers ask when they're thinking about a ROWE for their team or organization. These questions are important because evolving to a ROWE requires a different way of solving common challenges. Lose no sleep! Here are the answers.

Q: Wait! Some people really like going into the office. Are you Saying "no offices"?

A: Not at all. We're saying think about the outcome you need to accomplish first, not a physical location first and then the outcome. True confession time: Jody and I are guilty of thinking about this in the wrong order. Our first thought when we separated from Best Buy to start operating independently as CultureRx was: "Where will our office be?" We started looking at properties and even had one selected that we liked best. As we toured the space with our team during a final walk-through, it dawned on us: we didn't need a location like that; we'd never use it. But we had been laboring under the belief that you need to have a permanent common space that everyone can use. We walked away from that space, and for the past 5 years, our organization has been operating with the world as our "office."

Now, obviously, there *are* some outcomes that will be tied to a physical location—and location is important for those. But don't become one of those organizations that focuses so much on physical location that you lose the opportunities that come from making work something you do, rather than someplace you go.

Q: Our clients like to see us in an office—not shopping— at 2:00.

A: This is true. And it's also crap. Think about it: your client would rather see you at a desk in an office staring straight ahead and dreaming about lying on a beach rather than shopping while coming up with the solution to the issue they've been trying to solve for 2 years. Over time, we've succumbed to, "Well, that's what the client wants to see, so we'll do it—even if it's not really providing the best service" . . . and even if it's killing our employees.

But let's not be too harsh on the clients or customers; after all, they're simply working off what they know. It makes them feel good to see you at your desk in the office because they equate that with good service. Anything else makes them uncomfortable. The question is, Do *you* want to continue doing what you know is going to impede your ability to move into the future? Or will you take this opportunity to gently retrain your clients on what good service *really* means?

Know that it won't be easy if you opt to gently retrain. Although we recommend taking this approach, our clients who do so generally endure some pain as they're rewiring clients' brains. However, there's a simple strategy to use with clients who try to draw you back into the twentieth century:

Client: Where is Jan?
You: Have you tried calling or e-mailing her?
Client: No, I just thought she'd be here, so I stopped by.
You: Give her a call or shoot her an e-mail. She'll be happy to assist with whatever you need.

Client: Well, when do you expect her back?

You: She'll take care of anything you need—just reach out to her.

Expect a little pain as you use this approach, but know that in the end, your organization will actually operate better and more efficiently against client needs—and clients *will* recognize that.

Q: Some people need to be managed and like structure.

A: "Some people like to have me breathing down their neck, telling them when they can use the restroom, rejecting their vacation requests, and identifying a good time for lunch. Some people just like that." Really? Really?! And some people just like me to poke them in both eyes with rusty nails, too.

Actually, our favorite quote along these lines is, "Well, let's face it. Jack is only a grade level 6. Those people aren't really capable of operating with this kind of freedom." We're not even going to waste our breath here explaining how demeaning and demoralizing that is. If you're a manager who has said something like that in the past, we forgive you—but don't let it happen again.

Do some people like structure? Sure, they do. But they can decide that for themselves—and decide as well exactly what that structure needs to look like.

Do some people like to be managed? We're going out on a limb here, but we're going to say no. No one, anywhere, gets up and thinks, "I can't wait to be managed today." People do wake up and want to know how they're doing from a work perspective, how their performance is stacking up, and how they can improve. Always, always ask yourself whether you're focusing on managing the work or the people. If it's the people, your eye is on the wrong ball—and it's time to refocus.

Q: How do I determine what to pay part-time people?

A: This question can bring on some pretty intense pain. But it's a good sign if you're asking it, because it shows you're beginning to realize that part-time might not have a place in a ROWE. After all, part-time positions are all about how many hours, or how much time, someone is putting in. In a ROWE, of course, it's not about that at all; it's about the outcome you deliver.

We've had part-time employees who move into a ROWE say to their managers, "I should be able to go back to full-time salary because I'm still doing everything I was before but just in fewer days. And, I still find myself doing some work on my days off."

Traditionally, pay for someone who moves to or starts a part-time position is determined according to expected hours to be worked. Managers or organizations might not even address the actual workload. This is why workload is often never adjusted for people who go from full-time to part-time. The pay piece is adjusted only due to a change in the expectation of hours. People tend to accept this, because they view the new situation as one that gives them back some control over their life. But accepting less pay to do the same amount of work is a sick and twisted scenario.

The terms *full-time* and *part-time* won't exist in the future. Pay will instead be determined based on outcomes. For now, though—while we're in this agonizing limbo land where things can't change *too* fast—make sure you're determining whether workload or expected outcomes will change when adjusting pay for any reason. Time does not play into that equation, so don't let it creep in.

Q: How am I going to know if the people can get the work done if I don't do time estimates?

A: It's important to involve the team in conversations about outcomes and deadlines. It's not up to you to determine whether the people can get the work done. It's a joint effort between you and your employees to come to an agreement on what the outcome is, how it will be measured, and what the deadline is. Then it's up to your team to deliver. You should have the conversation about whether the deadline is unreasonable up front. Another option is to renegotiate the deadline, because other factors might come into play as the work process unfolds.

Time estimates do nothing but set up a weak expectation that people use as their guide, instead of using the outcome and customer expectations.

Q: I don't trust a system that's just a free-for-all. What about ethical behavior and making sure people are living our values? Does a ROWE just do away with all of that?

A: In a ROWE, people murder one another. They steal. They lie. They cheat. All the time. Every day. It's INSANE.

We've always wanted to say that in response to this question. A ROWE is most certainly *not* a free-for-all. It's an environment of responsibility and accountability, for the results and to one another. You should assume that people who are hired into an organization are trustworthy, ethical human beings; otherwise, you wouldn't have hired them. Adhering to organizational values is the ticket in.

Do a few people slip through the cracks? Yes. You might have some folks working with you who are a little less than stellar in the values category. If they're going to lie, cheat, and steal, they're going to do that whether or not you've moved into a ROWE. It's who they are. The advantage to a ROWE is that you'll spot their behavior much more quickly. They won't be able to hide because you'll be watching their outcomes, and unethical behavior will stand out in a big way. Not to mention that people start protecting the organization much more intensely in a ROWE. If coworkers in more of a traditional environment know that someone is stealing, they might think, "More power to them. If I could get away with it, I'd steal from this hellhole, too." In a ROWE, people are grateful for the autonomy they have and the lives they're able to live. So they call out the person who is acting in an unethical manner, because they don't want the organization to be hurt.

Things to Try

1. If you haven't already, read *Why Work Sucks and How to Fix It*, the manifesto of a ROWE.

(continued)

(*continued*)

2. Challenge your brain to think about *work* as a verb. Work is something you *do*, no matter where you physically *are*.

3. Next time you hear someone say, "So-and-so's teleworking," examine your own use of useless labels about work location. Now, stop using them. Replace the language with a statement about the *work*.

4. Change your next "flexibility" conversation to a "performance" conversation.

5. Grocery shop on a Tuesday before 5 PM.

Things to Avoid

1. Paying for people's mobile phones and home Internet. *So* past century.

2. Implementing an unlimited vacation policy on top of your current culture.

3. Paying nonexempt employees less money if they get their work done in less than 40 hours. Why would you punish them if the work is accomplished?

4. Managing by walking around. Let people *work*.

5. Tracking time or talking about number of hours worked with exempt-status employees.

Get Support!

Go to www.gorowe.com-books-and-tools to download a twenty-first century handbook that's ROWE approved.

Creating an Accountability Culture

by Karren Fink

Karren Fink is the senior vice president, human resources, at Edmunds.com, Inc. Edmunds.com, Inc., is a Santa Monica–based company that publishes free car-shopping tools, including car prices, projected ownership costs, car reviews, and car dealer inventory listings, as well as automotive consumer advice articles, such as its renowned "Confessions of a Car Salesman" series. Each month, approximately 18 million people use Edmunds.com's award-winning site and apps to research cars and automotive issues. The company is regularly recognized as a "Best Place to Work."

Edmunds.com started its journey to a Results-Only Work Environment (ROWE) with CultureRx's on-site training in February 2011. Since then, through a series of on-site training workshops, the company has established a ROWE within its entire organization.

Over the past several decades, the image of "work" has been carefully ingrained into American culture: "clock in" at the office at 9 AM, attend a meeting or two, break for lunch, and continue chugging along until the magical 5 PM hour (or, in most industries and companies, even later), at which time you're free to resume your personal life. And we accept this schedule, by and large, because that's just how work has always been done in most corporate environments.

But anyone who's been a member of the professional world since before the turn of this century

(*continued*)

(*continued*)

knows that we often get our work done at a variety of hours by using a variety of technologies. We could literally do our work 24/7. It's also clear these days that some work can be done without ever stepping foot in the office. Mobile technology has made it just as easy to respond to an e-mail message from a grocery store aisle as from a desktop computer. Analysts can present the same charts and graphs from several time zones away as if they were in the same room as the audience. We certainly still need to collaborate and build relationships to increase effectiveness and produce continual innovation, but we all know that the world of work has changed. Today's workers demand both flexibility and ownership of their time. They are just as dedicated—if not more so—to getting work done; they just don't want to be confined to the traditional norms to do so.

This evolving workplace is not lost on our human resources (HR) team at Edmunds.com. Our employees' needs go far beyond 401(k) packages and medical plans. They are craving environments that allow them the freedom to decide the appropriate work/life balance for themselves while fulfilling their obligations to the company.

To stay competitive, we've long strived to keep an external focus and, as such, are influenced by strategic business thinkers. One day in 2010, the Edmunds.com chairman came to me after reading Charlene Li's *Open Leadership*. He shared an excerpt that focused on Netflix's efforts to eliminate rules and policies that get in the way of achieving excellence. The excerpt focused on how eliminating the company's vacation policy was in keeping with the company's culture: they don't track how much they work, so why would they track how much time they didn't work? Our chairman suggested that since this approach seemed to be consistent with our culture as well, we should further investigate how it might fit with our own company. The insinuation was that if we give our employees the liberty to take time off as needed, they would deliver all that they are accountable for—and more.

It was the latter part that left me feeling a little uneasy. Maybe it was my "old HR goblins" coming out, but I felt we needed to ensure that we had a culture of accountability before we could eliminate a vacation policy. I feared the extreme: no controls may lead to work not getting done at all. I felt we needed to focus on both sides of the liberty and accountability equation.

After researching more on this topic, I was fascinated by the work that Best Buy had done in this area. Its focus on results coupled with working "whenever, wherever" was intriguing to me. That's

(continued)

(*continued*)

how I grew acquainted with the folks at CultureRx and the concept of a ROWE. Although I thought the concepts were interesting—and that they could help us reach the cultural and policy goals we were seeking—I didn't want it to be a typical "HR policy initiative." I wanted this to be a business initiative that we felt compelled to implement to ensure we were attracting and retaining top talent.

Our chief information officer (CIO) had also been exposed to similar encouragement from our chairman on this topic. As such, he could see the value in what a program like this could do for attracting top information technology (IT) talent (a competitive talent market anywhere, but particularly in Southern California). He was eager to test this out and recommended two of his teams to pilot a ROWE and evaluate the pilot's success against three criteria:

1. Are we meeting results?
2. Do the employees like it?
3. Is it generating buzz in other parts of the company?

It didn't take long for us to get our answers. The teams regularly finished their projects ahead of schedule, which allowed them to tackle even more objectives. Employees felt a more powerful sense of pride in the work they accomplished, while at the same time reporting a more effective work/life balance. And others in the company took notice, especially as our CIO shared with other department leaders how satisfied he was with his teams' performances.

We took another three teams through the pilot with similar results. At that point, we knew we had "tested" enough and were ready to make the leap. Within 18 months from the first pilot, we rolled out ROWE into every part of our company.

Often times I find that an outsider's first reaction to a ROWE is, "Wow, that's really cool that you offer so much independence." And then that sentiment is almost always followed up with, "So it's a workplace that actually treats you like an adult!" This latter reaction strikes to the core of what makes a ROWE so successful: treat your employees like adults, and they will behave like adults.

But transitioning to a ROWE does not come without challenges. Perhaps above all else, ROWE participants need to always keep one theme in mind: results are king. It is not a *Remote*-Only Work Environment. Everyone is accountable for the results they are expected to achieve. Much of these changes, of course, start at the top, and it is important for department leaders to embrace these

(continued)

(continued)

cultural transformations and reinforce them to their teams.

By instituting a ROWE, we've taken one giant step toward distinguishing ourselves from other companies, something that has allowed us to be more competitive in recruiting top talent. A ROWE also offers us the flexibility to eliminate the geographic restrictions in our recruiting process, which in turn allows us to consider the brightest and most motivated candidates, no matter where they're based. But there's also the huge perk of the freedom to avoid a commute at the height of rush hour for our local employees, especially in a city like Los Angeles, where Edmunds.com's headquarters office is located.

Oh, and by the way, we also changed our vacation policy to one that no longer considers formulas, tracking, or arbitrary limits. Our time away from work policy fits hand in hand with a ROWE: take time off whenever you need and want, as long as the work is covered.

What makes Edmunds.com such a unique and innovative company is our desire to fearlessly approach new ideas and mold them to suit the best interest of both our customers and the staff that serves them. Our shift to a ROWE fits perfectly within that philosophy. And even though we're still in the relative infancy of a ROWE, we feel we've already taken the lead to usher in a new era of workplace culture that motivates employees to take more ownership and accountability.

And that's one result that we *all* want to see.

2

Motivate Me

No Pizza Party, Please

A s we were thinking about writing the sequel to *Why Work Sucks and How to Fix It*, we realized that we could take a number of directions. But in the end, we knew this book had to be about how to truly make a Results-Only Work Environment (ROWE) come to life—and, perhaps most important, how to be a successful manager in that environment. The word *manager* comes with so much baggage that it's going to take a lot of work to emerge from under all of that and get centered around a new framework for "managing" that will truly allow members of organizations to succeed in ways we might never have imagined. There have been many

management theories and fads. This chapter will sim-
plify some main points so you'll understand them to be
able to put them into practice and reap the rewards.

When you think about that word—*manager*—there's
usually a negative connotation associated with it. For
decades, we've been associating that word with annoying
characters from comic strips (think the Pointy-Haired
Boss from *Dilbert*) and the "bad guy" in work-related
movies (think Bill Lumbergh from *Office Space:* "I'm
gonna need you to go ahead and come in on Saturday").
But for the person (maybe you) who *is* the manager, it
doesn't start out this way—at least not right at the very
beginning. People are usually at least temporarily excited
to get into a management role because it probably meant
a promotion, more compensation, and/or the subtle
message of "the organization trusts you to handle this
responsibility."

After the brief moment of basking in that sense of
accomplishment for landing a management role, however,
the realization sets in that there's more behind that
management curtain than you were expecting. Figuring
out how to keep your employees working for you when
they're unhappy, bringing up engagement scores that have
been steadily declining over the past 3 years, conducting
performance appraisals, dealing with vacation requests,
taking disciplinary action, terminating employment . . .
was this what you bargained for when you accepted the
position?!

So what happens next? More than likely, you're left
to figure it out on your own. Perhaps there's a mentoring
program at your organization where you've gathered some

good tips, or maybe you've attended some conferences that have shed light on areas that you've been wondering about. There are hundreds of management experts who try to impart their knowledge through various means; perhaps you've taken bits and pieces from these and worked them into your strategies. Sometimes it's hard to distill the lessons upon lessons of what makes a good manager into a bite-sized "Oooohh, this is what it's all about!" moment. We'll do that for you here, using our perspective, which is, we admit, a little different from that of your average management expert. The material we're going to cover in this chapter has been gathered from three angles, which is why we think you'll find it useful. First, we have the experiences of being employees, of working for managers who got it and for those who clearly didn't. We've seen, heard, and felt what works and what doesn't work from that perspective. We've sat in meetings where someone spoke the right words, and then experienced something a half hour later that made those words seem completely empty.

Second, we've been, and still are, managers ourselves. We know firsthand how difficult it is to focus on managing the work, and not the people. There is so much surrounding the manager-employee relationship *all* the time—and it's easy to veer off track and lose sight of the bigger picture.

Third, we have the experience of interacting with teams across the country over the past 9 years and moving them into a ROWE. Obviously, part of this has involved shifting thousands of managers into the twenty-first-century style of management, one that fosters increased productivity, higher levels of engagement, and better retention. We believe that all of these angles have granted us an extraordinary amount of knowledge that we're going to put into some key takeaways for you. Be prepared to have your "manager hat" blown off as you read on.

> Jody: I remember when we at CultureRx became a wholly owned subsidiary of Best Buy, Co., Inc., and the human resources (HR) vice president over our division at Best Buy said to us, "Just wait until you get employees. That's when it gets difficult." We know the challenge comes because everyone tries to manage the people, not the work, and we learned that one the hard way. But once we got clear on what we were *actually* managing, things got easier.

People often ask us, "What's the biggest challenge you've run across when working with teams to implement a ROWE?" Our response: "Management." To have a well-functioning ROWE, you need to have well-functioning managers, ones who understand, as we've said earlier, that it's not about managing the *people*, but managing the *work*. It's not about controlling the *how*; it's about making sure the *what* is clear and measurable and that people are accomplishing it.

Ronnie Wooten is president and chief operating officer at our client site Suntell. Financial Institution Technologies, Inc., d/b/a Suntell, was founded in 1996 by bankers. Suntell has made a focused commitment to delivering integrated commercial loan risk management software solutions to the banking industry. Wooten admits,

> Shifting from managing the people to managing the results was a major adjustment for me once we transitioned to ROWE. I viewed myself as a hands-off manager—prided myself in not micromanaging my staff. Shortly after the transition to ROWE, however, it quickly became evident to me that my staff was afraid to make a decision—they looked to me to make every decision and dictate every move. I realized I was a control freak. In order for ROWE to be successful, I had to stop [these tendencies] and instead guide this staff of highly knowledgeable, greatly experienced professionals into feeling secure in making their own decisions. This part wasn't that difficult; most of them readily accepted the responsibility, as they understood that with freedom comes responsibility. But as they needed me less and less, in terms of daily guidance and *bossing*, I began to feel a loss—of my position, my power, and my necessity within the company structure. I battled with the thought that perhaps I just wasn't needed any longer. I mean, if everyone could think on their own and make good decisions—and I didn't need to track their time or boss them around anymore—how could the company justify continuing to pay my salary? I grieved this loss until one day it occurred to me: I am the mentor. [My role is] to guide, to reassure, to help these people grow professionally.

Once I embraced that change in my role, I found that I enjoyed being a manager more than I ever had in the 20 years I'd been in management. I now find my position to be the most fulfilling it has ever been. I have passed the torch to the ones *doing*, have learned so much and have relished in their successes and ideas. To know that they have brought our company to the next level because I believed in them and allowed them to use their *adult* minds and knowledge to do so makes me more proud than I have ever been.

As managers with whom we've worked will attest to, this is much harder than it sounds. There comes a first moment of truth during our sessions with managers on the road to ROWE implementation when the lightbulb goes off about what a ROWE really is. It's *truly* an environment where people are free to do whatever they want, whenever they want, as long as they get their work done. When managers' minds click with this, someone always raises his or her hand to ask, "But . . . how will we know what people are *doing* in an environment like that?" Our response (because this is such an important, fundamental, and frequently received question) is, "How do you know now?" And here is where the spotlight begins shining on the real problem: they *don't* know. They admit that they know when people are coming to the office, how much time they spend at their desks, how long their lunch breaks are, who is taking vacation when, and how many sick days everyone has. But when they have to answer the question of whether the work is getting done, they don't know how to. Instead of managing the work, they've been monitoring the hallways and focusing on areas that end up derailing performance rather than improving it.

The following sections discuss some common rabbit holes that managers might find it easy to slip into while trying to manage the work instead of the people.

Scenario #1

Vice president of ABC Company: I'm concerned about the level of teamwork in your group. I used to see people congregating all the time in the lunchroom to talk and catch up. I haven't seen that lately, and that worries me.

Manager: I don't really think the level of teamwork has gone down . . .

Vice president: Well, I'm not feeling the energy I used to from the group—and we count on that for new ideas and fresh perspectives. How about we institute a core day when everyone needs to come into the office— just to be sure we're encouraging that camaraderie?

Manager's response:

a. Okay, that sounds good. Which day should we select?
b. I'll think about that.
c. Have you noticed any slips in our customer satisfaction levels?

If you answered (c), you're managing the work . . . and helping educate *your* boss about focusing on results. Making assumptions about what things look like around you may or may not have anything to do with the quality of the work, customer satisfaction levels, or innovation probability. The questions need to center on the *work*, not how often people are seen interacting with one another.

Scenario #2

Vice president of ABC Company: I've heard that Cara is going to start doing some work at home. I know she has two small children. Have you made sure to ask her if she has child care lined up for them since we'll need her to be working from 8 to 5, not tending to their needs?

Manager: Well, I haven't asked her that, but I assume she'll do what she needs to.

Vice president: I've seen too many of these situations in the past where the work doesn't get done. Please address it as soon as possible.

Manager's response:

a. Consider it done. I'll talk with her first thing tomorrow.

b. Let's see how it goes; maybe there won't be any issues.

c. It sounds like you're worried about Cara not delivering. She and I are very clear about her goals and how they will be measured. If her performance slips, I will address that—just like I would with any of our employees.

Again, if you answered (c), you're in good shape. Directing the conversation back to the work and stressing that you'll handle performance issues if they arise is critical. It's not about what employees are doing every second of every day; it's about whether they're delivering what the organization needs.

Scenario #3

Vice president of ABC Company: I just heard from our biggest client that he was here the other day and said this place was a ghost town. That is not the image I want to portray to the client who's bringing in more than a quarter of our revenue this year.

Manager: I'm sure it wasn't a "ghost town." You know how he tends to overexaggerate.

Vice president: Overexaggeration or not, we will have our employees here to serve our clients. When is our next all-hands meeting so that we can make sure this message gets out there?

Manager's response:

a. I think it's next Monday. Should I get it on the agenda?

b. I'm not sure this is a good idea. Maybe we can find out who *was* here and let him know that the office wasn't *totally* empty?

c. I'd actually like to have a conversation with the client and make sure he's getting everything he needs from us. We just did a customer satisfaction survey with his company where our team scored a 4.92 out of 5. If there's something we're not providing, I'd like to know about it.

There's that (c) again. Retraining client perceptions is another opportunity in a ROWE. Organizations often find themselves sinking into behaviors that they don't necessarily agree with simply to please the customer or client. Some of those behaviors might be okay, but when they come at the cost of your employee engagement levels, for instance, it's time to ensure the client knows you're focused on delivering results—that's a constant.

■ ■ ■

So how can we ensure that the switch from managing the people to managing the work is accomplished in a deliberate, successful manner?

First, as we've said time and again, one of the biggest, most dangerous management traps is focusing on time. It's easy to watch when people come in and when they leave. And, sadly, those have become major cornerstones of determining whether employees are delivering—not delivering the work, but delivering their time. If they're doing this by showing up (during the right times of day and in the right location), then managers assume that the right work must be happening, too. It's a false assumption, of course, but it's become an anchor for managers. Time and physical presence provide a sense of security. When everyone is at his or her cube at 8 AM, that's a mark that the day has started off well. If five people *aren't* in their cubes by that time, the mission of the old-world manager is to find out where they are. And, when they do come in, to find out why they weren't in "on time." Not only that, but they believe that it's necessary to make sure those employees know that they're expected to arrive no later than 8 AM or there will be consequences. The conversation typically isn't about the work, but just a simple, "I need to see you every morning by 8 AM."

Focusing on time lets everyone in an organization continue playing the game: working more hours, not taking lunch, bragging about how much vacation time they have banked by not taking their days. The focus is on all of *that*, rather than where it should be: on producing results and gaining ground on, or surpassing, your competition. You can lay out all the right strategies for succeeding as an organization, hire consultants to help you achieve your business goals, launch well-thought-out initiatives, but it's all for naught if you reward time. We've had clients tell us that before moving to a ROWE, there was unhealthy competition among employees who were always trying to out-time each other and be the one who got the manager's praise. They knew they had to be the first one in the parking lot, the one who talked about skipping lunch, the one who sent e-mails out at midnight, the one who came into the office sick. Employees pick up on all of this quickly. And whether they're achieving anything meaningful, they notice that these are the types of things managers notice, even if only in subtle ways. "Nancy, you were up late last night—got that e-mail from you at 1 AM! You must be tired this morning!" Joe, who happened to be sitting right next to Nancy when these comments were relayed, heard this: "I love when people show their dedication by working at night (outside of 'office hours'). When I see people with dark circles under their eyes, it means they're giving it all they've got." Interestingly, you'll never hear a manager say, "Nancy, got that e-mail from you at 11 AM! Did you send that before lunch?" Managers give their attention to e-mails sent outside of traditional office hours, which is what sets the tone for what employees *think* they need to do, even if it's setting their e-mails to go out at certain times of the night just so they can reap some praise for their dedication to the work.

Part of what managers in a ROWE want to do is encourage *healthy* competition that's improving the results being delivered to customers. The goal is to remove any basis for the games involving time as a means to gain your attention. It is critical to make it clear, through your actions and behavior, that you value results and customer satisfaction. Here are some statements to *avoid* if you want to end the time games:

"I think we should take a minute to call out Tom at our next meeting. He cancelled that trip he had scheduled with his family to complete the project for XYZ client. He deserves some recognition for that."

"Sharon, I saw your car here bright and early this morning! No problem finding a parking spot at that hour, right?!"

"John, you probably have no idea how busy rush hour traffic is during the afternoons since you're always hard at work here after the rest of the team takes off!"

"That new deli section in the cafeteria is great! But Teresa wouldn't know about that—she's hard at work even through lunch, right, Teresa?!"

Jody: At the old Best Buy Campus in Eden Prairie, Minnesota, we knew who the slackers were. They were the ones who parked in the "loser lot"—the lot so far away from the building you practically had to hail a taxi if you were wearing anything but thigh-high boots in the winter or running shoes in the summer. Forget the Manolo Blahniks, girls. Anyone who got to work later than 7:45 AM was a "loser." It was the hobble of shame, that's for sure.

When employees don't have to worry about being recognized for these things anymore, it gives everyone more energy to get on the same page with the results. Instead of seeing who can come in earlier and stay later, employees compete to make sure the organization wins, which is exactly where their focus should be.

Many managers believe they're already fostering this.

But this is also where a lot of mangers get tripped up. You can say the right things: "I don't care when you come and go. Do whatever you need to do!" But then you get anxious, because some people need you to set boundaries for them, right? If you leave the door wide open like that, they might overwork themselves; they won't be able to decide for themselves when to stop. And isn't that what a caring manager does—help people figure that out? In response to your anxiety, you find yourself saying things like:

"You've been working so hard over the past few weeks. Why don't you take Friday off?"

"It's 6 PM already. You should knock off and go be with your family!"

"They're predicting snow this afternoon. Why don't you guys take off at 3 PM?"

"With your sister sick in the hospital, you probably shouldn't be working while you're there. Just take time to be with her. I don't want to see any e-mails from you!"

At first glance, all of these statements look like they're meant to help employees find work/life balance, set boundaries, even keep them safe. However, think about these in a different way. In the new world of management we've been discussing in this book, you're trying to set a tone of letting *your employees* decide how they'll get their work done. You want them to make commonsense decisions about that and let them know that you trust them to make the right decisions. So let's review these statements with a glimpse into what might be going through your employees' minds when you make them:

"You've been working so hard over the past few weeks. Why don't you take Friday off?"

Employee's internal interpretation: "Oh, I was planning to not do any work on *Thursday*. Now I should probably change my plans since it sounds like he wants me to take Friday instead."

■ ■ ■

"It's 6 PM already. You should knock off and go be with your family!"

Employee's internal interpretation: "Am I not spending enough time with my family? I was planning to stay and finish this stuff up so I could go to the zoo with the kids tomorrow morning, but maybe I should just go home now and come in tomorrow morning . . ."

■ ■ ■

"They're predicting snow this afternoon. Why don't you guys take off at 3 PM?"

Employee's internal interpretation: "I heard that prediction, too, and I was planning to take off at 11 AM. I guess I'll just stay and hope the snow doesn't get too bad by 3 . . ."

■ ■ ■

"With your sister sick in the hospital, you probably shouldn't be working while you're there. Just take time to be with her. I don't want to see any e-mails from you!"

Employee's internal interpretation: "If my sister is sleeping and I want to do some e-mails, will she think I'm ignoring her? Will my boss think I'm a cold-hearted sibling? Doing some work was going to be the one thing that might save my sanity during this ordeal. . . ."

To ensure that employees feel totally at ease making their own decisions about how they approach the work every day, these statements need to go. It's not up to you, as a manager, to figure out someone's work/life balance equation or keep him or her safe. It's not that you don't care about your employees, but you need to care first and foremost that the work is getting done.

Jody: It's somewhat painful for me to remember when Cali had her third child (okay, she has *four!*) and was in the hospital. It's her third. She's chillin'. We're e-mailing. Baby is born. Baby sleeps *a lot* at the hospital. Cali and I are still communicating because her brain isn't shut off. We're talking about lives, babies, and well . . . work stuff. Imagine our dismay when, without even telling her, HR found out the day she delivered and automatically deducted 48 hours from her vacation bank. And then, even though she continued to respond to business needs— and work with me to make business decisions—she suddenly saw her paychecks being reduced by 40 percent. She needed to be bonding with her baby after all. She can't possibly be contributing "full time." I was so raving mad I'm surprised I had enough wherewithal to be calm when I went to HR to set the record straight.

We know that it can be scary to let go this much— really scary. Will the work get done if you truly leave the *how* up to employees? Will they do the right things? What if they don't? These worries can lead to an urge to give the best performers more and more to do. You start to identify those you can consistently count on to go above and beyond and those become your go-to people. Since Jill can really crank it out, why not give her more? She's efficient, productive, and really knows what she's doing, so there's nothing wrong with that . . . or is there?

Think about it this way: You and your peer are both responsible for achieving X by June 30. You achieve it by June 19 and feel great, because you delivered before the deadline. You figure you'll have a chance to breathe before the next project comes down the pike. Your peer delivers right on the deadline of June 30. In the meantime, you were given another project that has the same due date of June 30. Your efficiency was rewarded with . . . more work. On July 1, you're both given another project with a deadline of July 31. What have you learned? Better to eke it out and not submit anything until July 31 . . . or you might find yourself in the same boat you were in during June with just getting more work.

This is a common behavior among managers. There's a lot of work to accomplish; why *not* find the people who can deliver quickly and efficiently and give them more? Because this approach undermines the efficiency you *could* experience. Remember that time game we just talked about? This is another game employees learn to play. We've heard from more than one client site that employees have told their peers to "slow down," because they're making others on the team look bad. When managers get wind of this, they deal with it by saying (again, the right words), "We *want* efficiency in our work. This is what we strive for!" But giving more work to the efficient employees negates the words. After all, no one wants to be rewarded with more work.

So then the question for a manager becomes, "How will we get all the work done if I can't give it to the efficient performers?" Would you believe us if we told you that, in a ROWE—when people are rewarded for efficiency with time versus more work—they start asking for more to do? Didn't think so. Most managers don't see how that can happen. Tara Leitner is managing content editor at our client WATT Publishing. Established in 1917, WATT is a media company that provides business-to-business knowledge and information to the agribusiness industry. As Leitner explains, "We bring buyers and sellers in the poultry, pig, feed, and pet food industries together with our leading content distributed through a wide array of media channels."

Leitner has seen employees in a ROWE be completely okay with taking on more work firsthand:

> As I was having a discussion with one of my employees about what she wanted to work on, a couple of new goals formed organically [as a result of] talking about the company's strategic plan, and she was excited and motivated to work on them. More work? In a sense, yes. But that's the powerful [thing that happens] when you stop thinking about work as time and tasks, and start seeing the results as the end game. [These employees] won't be working some insane amount of hours to complete these goals; we set reasonable expectations for

them, and I know they'll get done and the results from them will offer value to WATT. This is the exciting cycle of motivation among employees— and what more could I ask for in a team? I look forward to encouraging that cycle through coaching and leadership.

Leitner brings up a great point about employee motivation. Typically, managers' conversations about how to motivate employees center on compensation, tangible rewards, and other extrinsic inputs. As we know from the research that author Daniel Pink has relayed in *Drive*, intrinsic motivation levels really matter—making the shift from needing "stuff" to make you feel like you want to perform well to knowing that, if you perform well, you're achieving larger goals for society and for your life. But intrinsic motivation can't really emerge when the manager is in the role of *prescribing* how work will happen.

Perhaps the greatest fear for a manager who really *does* want to let go of this control is handling employees who *don't* deliver their results. This fear even ends up keeping managers from adopting a ROWE, because they're paralyzed by the notion of actually having to deal with these employees. On one hand, this is understandable; these are difficult conversations to have. On the other hand, organizations exist for a reason, and people who work in them are paid to deliver results. There needs to be consequences when that doesn't happen.

We've had countless conversations with teams in organizations when we've asked the question, "What happens if you don't achieve your results?" Know what we hear? Silence. Complete silence. Everyone looks at one another, and then they all look down at their laps. They're either afraid to talk about the consequences, or they have no idea what they are. Or worse yet, they have no idea what the results are that they're supposed to work *toward*, never mind the consequences. This is a sign of an organization that's not focused in the right direction. Organizations that have a clear focus on results have done two things:

1. They've made those results and associated measures very clear to employees (and employees have bought in to them).

2. They've fostered a culture of accountability and ownership in which employees are able to verbalize what will happen when they achieve their results— and when they don't.

It's a problem if you can hear a pin drop when posed the question, "What happens if you don't achieve your results?" In a ROWE, the loud and clear response from employees is, "No results, no job." They understand that they are receiving a paycheck as a reward for producing results, not putting in time, being in the right place, or making an effort.

Claiming to be focused on results but then not executing consequences doesn't work. The walk doesn't match the talk. But often, that's not on purpose. Managers *want* to give people a chance; they start justifying why employees aren't performing. They tell themselves that it's more trouble to hire someone new and train them, so they just make do. But all this does is lay the foundation for a lot of inner team turmoil.

In one of the direct health care settings where we conduted trainings, we talked with employees about what was holding them back from doing their best work. They cited a number of things, but we all knew that there was a big white elephant in the room the whole time they were rattling things off. Finally, a brave soul opened her mouth and said, "I'll tell you what's holding us back. Management won't fire the dead weight." Once that was out in the open, everyone in the room agreed. They described it like this: "We could have 15 people working a shift. Management thinks, 'You have 15 people working that shift. Why aren't you getting everything done?' In actuality, we could get more accomplished with 12 people than we can with 15 because we have 3 people who are taking up space and holding the rest of us back."

The lack of consequences in any system will hurt the whole, and this is where a lot of managers fall short. We've heard countless managers try to rationalize why they haven't taken action on employees they know aren't performing. We know it's not easy to take action. But our advice is this: take it anyway. And that doesn't necessarily mean terminating people who aren't performing. However, you *do* need to follow a consistent process when performance is suffering.

We have found that small organizations and family-owned businesses have a particularly difficult time with this consequences piece of things. The "family atmosphere" is often very much alive in these settings, which

sometimes works in the organization's favor and sometimes works against it. People may have been working
together for a very long time; perhaps many of them live
in the same town where they see each other on a daily
basis outside of the work setting. This adds another element of difficulty to the performance conversations. This
was the case at the Prairie Lakes Area Education Agency
(PLAEA), our client in the small town of Pocahontas,
Iowa. Connie Johnson, director of marketing and communication for PLAEA, says,

> We work alongside people who have lives and
> interests outside of work and [who] have built strong
> friendships with our coworkers. Many of us live in
> the same communities and we see each other when
> we're getting groceries, at a ball game, the movies,
> etc. Moving to a ROWE is helping us maintain
> those relationships because we can have separate
> conversations about performance and personal lives.
> In our Results-Only Work Environment, we're
> moving toward a peer-review system as one piece of
> the evaluation process. We believe it helps balance
> the feedback so it's not just one person's point of
> view or judgment. When all is said and done, I
> believe you don't have to have a relationship to get
> results. I believe that if you deliver results for the
> customer or colleague, a relationship will be built.

Couldn't have said it better ourselves!

Perhaps the biggest "Yeah, but" we hear about
delivering consequences in a work environment is
"Yeah . . . but what about in *unionized* environments?

Surely, there must be many, many hurdles to overcome? Can it even be done?" Our first reaction is usually to think (not say, mind you): "So it's okay to *not* deliver results in union shops?" Interestingly, in one union shop where we conducted training, one of the union stewards approached our trainer following the workshop and said, "What you're doing here with ROWE is taking away people's rights, and I don't like it one bit." You can imagine how this took our trainer aback! ROWE taking *away* people's rights? We'd never heard *that* one before. We usually hear quite the opposite, that ROWE is liberating people and giving them back freedoms they never should have lost in the first place. It became clear after more conversation that this particular union steward was of the belief that it's a right to have a job . . . regardless of whether you deliver results. The opportunities to deliver, in his mind, should be limitless, and taking away someone's job for failing to do so was simply wrong. Chew on that!

We witnessed the other end of the union spectrum when we worked with a group that experienced the ease of transitioning someone out of the organization when results are the focus. Anne Becker is general counsel and director of HR at our client Intermediate School District 287. They provide more than 120 programs and services to meet the most challenging educational needs of its 12 member school districts in suburban Minneapolis, Minnesota. District 287 operates six schools that each year educate nearly 3,000 full-time students who have significant special education needs or who are at risk of not graduating from high school. The district also offers a variety of part-time student options, including Career and

Technical education and Northern Star Online, the state's largest online learning consortium. In addition to the student programs, District 287 manages large-scale professional development and provides consultative services to school staff in education specialty areas. Anne shares the following:

> Supervisors and human resources staff may be concerned about the effect that moving to a ROWE could have on addressing ongoing employee performance issues in a unionized workplace. This was the case with a local government unit that piloted a ROWE beginning in 2011 with a group of employees, all of whom belonged to a union. Among this group was a long-time employee who was on a performance improvement plan and had been subjected to several progressive discipline steps over the course of the previous year. The employee's supervisor and the HR director expressed concern that moving to a ROWE might result in returning to "square one" with this employee, as he might argue that expectations were changing and he needed more time to adapt his performance to meet them.
>
> The ROWE consultant working with the organization explained that the process the supervisor and employees would complete to clearly articulate the expectations for the positions involved in the pilot would *assist* in the performance improvement effort, rather than set it back. She explained that when employees are in a ROWE, it is much easier to use objective measurement to tell whether an employee is achieving the necessary results.

Not long after the group had determined the desired results—as well as the method for measuring success in achieving them—the employee in question decided to leave the organization. In the end, moving to a ROWE not only did not delay the performance improvement process; it actually accelerated the desired result: encouraging an employee who was not meeting expectations to move on without the need for a lengthy grievance process or arbitration hearing.

Not only have managers been squirming about performance conversations for decades, so have employees. Most employees hate it when performance appraisal time rolls around. They start figuring out what their goals have been (or should have been) for the previous year so that they can fill in their appraisal paperwork. Their stomachs become increasingly knotted as the day of the appraisal approaches because they're so filled with angst about what the conversation will be like. Sweating bullets, they arrive to the conversation, ready for anything. And what can really make the sweat start to drip during the dreaded hour-long meeting is when managers have one version of how they think employees have performed throughout the year and employees have another.

It doesn't have to be this way.

Janelle Riley is chief executive officer of our client Syvantis Technologies, which provides cloud-based technology solutions for businesses, freeing employees to work from anywhere, anytime. Riley shares that performance conversations aren't meant to be trips to hell and back:

Everyone at our company—managers and individual contributors—used to just hold their breath leading up to, and probably even during, performance reviews. They were this point in time during the year that no one wanted any part of. When we transitioned to a ROWE, we realized a couple of things about these conversations. First, they are critical to our success as a company, so having people dreading them and wishing for them to be over was dangerous to our health as a business. Second, we realized that it's all about performance in a ROWE. A review shouldn't be a once-a-year event. We naturally evolved to this place where we're having performance conversations every single day. We're always talking about where our results are headed, how metrics are looking, and how our customers are responding—all the time. Another huge thing we've done is make sure that all of our goals are objective, rather than subjective in nature. I think we used to get into situations where the goals were not only unclear, [but] there weren't any ways to measure them. This caused a lot of unnecessary stress during reviews. Now, everything is objective, and that's made a big difference."

Jody: I remember the stress of not only having to go through the painful experience of performance appraisals but the added stress of the nine-box rating system. I'd be sitting in a room with a bunch of

leaders who were talking about me and my performance and rating me on whether or not I'm living
the values of the company. Really? Most of them
don't even know me. They've never talked to me.
They have no clue as to my skill set, real capabilities,
or passions. They're relying on what my manager is
saying about me, and he's on a shaky foundation and
worried about his own advancement. To make it
even worse, I don't even really understand my
measurable results. In fact, the S.M.A.R.T. goals I
had crafted 10 months prior to the performance
appraisal event weren't even relevant anymore (find
out why in the next chapter!). But I sure talked about
how great I did on them. Does this create a little
anxiety? I guess so. Since it's so incredibly and
undeniably broken.

It's not that you have to dictate to your employees
that you will be having performance conversations with
them every day from this moment on. You'll notice
that Riley said, "we naturally evolved to this place." That
evolution occurs when you eliminate the safety net of
time and physical presence. Once managers and
employees realize those parameters can't, and won't, be
used as markers of good performance, everyone at every
level gets a little anxious. They *want* to be very clear
about what they need to deliver and how they will be
measured. Once that's in place, employees will take
the initiative to keep managers informed about how they're

progressing, how things are going, and whether they need assistance. That's right: *employees* will take the initiative. You won't need to worry about how they're doing or bug them for information; they'll be proactive about that. Why? Because they're focused on the outcome, and they're willingly and wholeheartedly invested in the organization's success.

Moving into this new way of thinking and operating might sound very appealing to a manager; however, it's crucial to remember that it's usually easier said than done. You may swing back and forth between the old world and a ROWE as you continue down the path. We've heard from many a manager that it can really help to express any anxiety you might have directly to your employees. To get you started on what you might say, run through these questions and reflect on them to identify what it is that you might really be nervous about:

- Do I believe that my employees are intrinsically motivated to perform versus feeling entitled to more and more given by the organization?
- Do I believe my employees understand that they are receiving a paycheck in return for achieving *measurable goals* that meet our customers'/clients' needs?
- Do I believe my employees support the fact that management will (and should) deal with performance-related issues swiftly?
- Do I believe that, once we're on the same page with outcome-based goals and measures, my employees will be up to the challenge of determining how to

approach the work in the most productive, efficient ways possible?

- Do I believe that I can confidently move out of my "babysitting" role and into that of coach, guide, and mentor?

- Do I have employees right now with whom I should be addressing performance?

You need to act upon anything you've identified after this self-reflection with your team. The more humility you display during this transition, the better. Your employees will only admire you for it. They'll realize that you're just a human being trying to move through this world of work, just as they are—and you're setting the tone with ROWE for amazing things to happen.

Shifting the platform that managers have been standing on for decades can be daunting, but it is completely necessary. Talking about how things need to change and acknowledging the reality of the situation has been a good admission . . . for the past 20 years. But there comes a point when it's time to move on from the "aha!" statement (which isn't so aha! anymore) to the solution, changing what it is that *management* means and what it focuses on.

Typical Questions

The following are typical questions managers ask when they're thinking about a ROWE for their team or organization. These questions are important because evolving to a ROWE requires a different way of solving common challenges. Lose no sleep! Here are the answers.

Q: I just don't trust some of my employees to operate this way.

A: If you don't trust some of your employees to achieve their results, why would you want them to continue working for you? Chances are, if you don't think they'll deliver, they probably *aren't* delivering now. Managing to results will expose those nonperformers *very* quickly. As they're exposed, you'll use what you learned earlier in this chapter and in Chapter 1 to move forward with a performance conversation.

Sometimes, managers experience the opposite of what they think will happen. You might not trust some employees to be able to deliver results. However, maybe they've felt stifled and constrained, and that's been prohibiting them from doing their best work. When you manage to results, you'll find that some employees who you were worried about rise to the top of the heap. Yes, it happens.

Q: What about people who need my supervision? They want it.

A: *noun*\, sü-pər-'vi-zhən\
    Definition of *SUPERVISION*
    : the action, process, or occupation of supervising; especially: a critical watching and directing (as of activities or a course of action)

After everything you've read so far in this book, we hope you'll see the absurdity of this definition. It falls into the old world of managing the people and the *how*. What does it really mean to be able to critically watch and direct activities if you never achieve the right results?

It's not your job to dictate how every little thing gets done throughout the day, the week, or the year. You're not a parent, or a babysitter. You are a results-focused manager—a guide, a mentor, and a coach. You're putting the control over the *how* into employees' hands and trusting that they'll deliver. And 95 percent of them will.

Some employees may say they need or want your supervision because they don't know anything different. They're accustomed to following orders and may feel lost in a world where *they* determine their next steps, instead of waiting for them to be handed down. This is where you must help employees see that the barometer of "doing a good job" is all about achieving measurable goals, which will be the main thing you're watching. As employees become more comfortable with the new approach, where they decide how to complete the work and you simply address their results, you'll hear less and less about any desire for supervision.

Q: I have some people who I'm afraid will never know when to stop working. What do I do about that?

A: This was something managers worried about in the old world. It was up to management to help put up the boundaries and stop people from overworking. This is where the comments we discussed earlier come into play: "It's 6 PM. Why don't you take off and get some rest?" In a ROWE, managers and employees agree on goals and measurements; how the employees go about achieving those is their own business. What might look like over-working to one person might be someone else's comfort zone. Similarly, what might look like slacking to one person might be someone else's perfect productivity zone. It's an employee's responsibility to initiate that conversation with you if he or she is feeling overworked.

Q: Does overachieving become the new standard?

A: The bar is continually pushed higher and higher in a ROWE. This isn't so much because employees want to outperform one another but because they are genuinely invested in the organization's success and want to see it continue to thrive. We've discussed unhealthy versus healthy competition in the work environment. Therefore, you probably understand by now that when you remove the factors that were generating unhealthy competition, you're left with a strong, healthy focus on the outcome of the organization. "I can do more" is a common statement in a ROWE. As a manager, you won't have to push people to go above and beyond; they're intrinsically motivated to do so.

Q: That's great that *some* employees will want to keep doing more. But what about people who never take on extra work?

A: This is yet another topic that can cause a lot of anxiety for managers. Often, they think it's their job to make things "fair." If you constantly see Robert and Cathy taking on more work because they want to, while Mark continues to do the "minimum," you feel like you need to fix that situation. But this isn't something you need to worry about in a ROWE because teams of employees will handle this situation themselves. When one employee simply won't ever take on or ask for more work in a ROWE, other team members will address it with that person. They'll put things in the perspective of the outcome for the organization and make it clear that everyone needs to play his or her part. If an employee still refuses, this is where the team starts operating like the television show *Survivor*. Everyone needs to step up to achieve the organization's goals—that is, survive on the island—or they will start to feel more and more pressure from their peers. This may necessitate a conversation with you, as the manager; however, you want to wait for it to come to you. Don't step in and intervene. If it does come your way, you simply may need to adjust the employee's performance goals. This will make the person aware of what needs to be achieved to meet expectations that are aligned with the rest of team and expected outcomes.

Q: What do I do if someone on the team isn't pulling his or her weight?

A: If "not pulling his or her weight" means not meeting results, a performance conversation is in order. If "not pulling his or her weight" means not picking up extra work, see the earlier discussion.

Things to Try

1. Express any anxiety you have about the *work* directly to your employee(s). For example, say, "I'm worried you may miss important deadlines."

2. Look for performance-related (measurable) outcomes achieved and recognize them.

3. Ask your employees to submit their ideas to solve a particular business challenge you are having (put a deadline on when you need their ideas).

4. Try working in locations other than the office building. And yes, we mean during what used to be "business hours."

5. Ask your employees how *they* would want to keep you apprised of how their work is progressing. You'll be surprised at the creative ways you'll be able to notice work happening.

Things to Avoid

1. Asking time-related questions that are schedule-based, such as, "When do you expect Jill to come in today?"

2. Recognizing employees for how much time they worked, how late they worked, or how early they came into the physical office.

3. Engaging in any conversation that traps you into making a decision about an employee's

schedule, such as, "Can I leave early today?"
This is not your decision anymore.

4. Doling out the work based on your perception
of who's the best performer.

5. Prescribing *how* work should get done.

Get Support!

Schedule a Beyond Telework for Managers
Workshop. Learn more by visiting www
.gorowe.com/training.

Join the ROWE Online Support Community. Learn
more by visiting www.gorowe.com/community.

The Importance of Trust

by Bryan Sivak

Bryan Sivak is the former chief technology officer of Washington, DC. The Office of the Chief Technology Officer (OCTO) is a 600-person cabinet agency of the government of the District of Columbia. OCTO's mission is to leverage the power of technology to improve service delivery, drive innovation, and bridge the digital divide to build a world-class city.

The mood in the conference room in the District of Columbia's Wilson Building—our city hall—was tense. Representatives from the mayor's office were looking for some answers, and although I'd provided as much detail as possible, there were still a number of unknowns that we couldn't comprehensively answer or commit to. *Would* a Results-Only Work Environment (ROWE) work in government? Well, I thought so, but I was unable to categorically state what the results would be. And because this kind of uncertainty is not traditionally built into government's DNA, moving to a ROWE was, in a sense, a grand experiment, with a big question mark punctuating the effort.

After a few months of work at my agency, the Office of the Chief Technology Officer (OCTO), we had just completed the first draft of our ROWE design document and were getting ready to start the rollout across this 600-person organization. There had been a number of peaks and valleys throughout the early stages of the process. We were prepared for this, given the magnitude of the changes we were about to unleash on the extremely proscriptive bureaucratic human resources processes typical to most government agencies.

What we *weren't* prepared for, however, was betrayal.

To make the process of implementation go a bit more smoothly, we had formed a 16-person ROWE design team. These individuals—comprised of a diagonal slice of individuals from every level across the agency—were partially selected by the leadership team and partially chosen by the agency staff themselves as representatives. Agency staff chose representatives based on three criteria: whom they trust, who gets things done, and who was already demonstrating the values of a ROWE. They met on a frequent basis through the early stages of the ROWE planning process to design the rollout, address employee concerns, and identify and solve for the issues specific to OCTO, as well as the DC government human resources (HR) regulations in general. We operated under a principle of complete transparency with respect to our activities, and the team acted as ambassadors to the rest of the agency. The team designed engagement strategies that included both formal and informal communications, including introducing ROWE at "all-staff" meetings. We had also consciously been conspicuously public with the effort, partnering with the Center for

(*continued*)

(*continued*)

American Progress' "Doing What Works" team in an effort to prevent any politically motivated accusations about employees "goofing off" or "wasting taxpayer dollars." Finally, I had kept our colleagues in the mayor's office and HR agency fully up to speed with our efforts.

We did keep one thing internal: a draft implementation strategy that would not be finalized or released until the staff had been fully engaged and had opportunities to shape, improve, and "own" it. The team agreed, as it needed employee vetting before it was completed, that it would not be shared with outside stakeholders until the internal work was complete.

As it turned out, one member of the design team was threatened by this change to the status quo and anonymously leaked our draft design document, along with some negative commentary, which resulted in a showdown at city hall. As we had all been working together very closely for a good amount of time, this news came as an emotional shock to the team and threatened to stop our efforts in their tracks. It wasn't just because we were prevented from doing the implementation; it was because this was a significant breach in the trust upon which we had based all our efforts.

Without trust, a ROWE is impossible. The *entire concept* of a ROWE is based on the recognition that individuals in the workplace are responsible adults who can be held accountable for their own high-quality production, which has nothing to do with where they are or how long they spend on a given task. This is even more true in a government bureaucracy, where the majority of the HR regulations are relics of a bygone era and are typically designed to prevent risk as opposed to embracing it and using that risk to advance the organization's efforts.

But this trust has to go both ways. Although it's necessary that managers fundamentally trust their employees, it's also critical for the rank and file to truly believe that leadership is on their side and has their back.

The design team worked both as a concept and in practice because the members were universally trusted and given autonomy by the leadership and had developed tight bonds between themselves. They were able to prove to the rest of the agency that senior leadership was serious about the effort—because they had the freedom to craft the implementation plans, answer questions honestly and publicly, and act on the tasks that had been identified and drawn up without management or oversight in true ROWE fashion.

And this is why the betrayal was such a blow. In an instant, the bonds of trust that had been built up among the design team were severely tested, and the

(continued)

(continued)

original attitude of "this will never work in government" started creeping back in.

At this point, as the head of the organization, I had a few choices. I could capitulate to the pressure and shut down the effort. I could launch a secret investigation to root out the troublemaker and administer punishment. Or I could gather the team to openly discuss what happened and see if we could resolve the issue.

As I pondered this choice, I realized that truly trusting my colleagues to the extent that a ROWE requires meant giving my staff the permission to betray *me*—and having faith that it wouldn't happen again. If we launched an investigation into the identity of the snitch, we would only be encouraging further distrust of one another.

So I chose the latter path. It wasn't easy. When I described to the design team the situation and what had happened, the sense of betrayal was palpable. The conversation that ensued was emotional and intense. These people had put their careers on the line for one another and every other agency employee, and they had been let down by one of their own.

But a remarkable thing happened next. Instead of giving up or starting to constantly look over their shoulders, the team doubled down on their efforts and resolved to make this happen—*whatever it took*. The level of intensity and personal involvement skyrocketed, and we were able to continue the process with a new level of understanding and, somewhat surprisingly, a closer team with much tighter bonds. And this drove our eventual solution to the concerns raised by the mayor's office. Instead of taking the traditional route of formally communicating our actions and plans from the agency head's perspective, we requested that individuals at *all* levels of the agency who would be impacted, positively or negatively, communicate their thoughts on the effort. These interactions spoke louder than any missive I could have drafted, and we were able to continue along our implementation path with a newfound sense of urgency and purpose.

Although we were eventually unable to finish the rollout due to the mayor's unsuccessful reelection bid, this incident reemphasized to me the fundamental importance of two-way trust in *any* relationship. Without the top-down and bottom-up trust granted to the design team, it would not have been possible to get as far as we did, especially given the potential negative consequences for the agency's individual employees. This led to a broader question and really the biggest takeaway from our experiment: What would be possible if we approached all

(continued)

(continued)

our relationships and activities with trust as our default setting? I believe the answer is simple: with trust as a solid foundation of our relationships and activities, we become collectively stronger teams, leveraging one another's talents, willing to take risks together, and notably, exceeding expected results.

CHAPTER

3

S.M.A.R.T. Goals = Senseless Minutia Against Random Tasks

This chapter is about shifting the focus away from workplace rules and policies that manage the people and toward a performance management style that manages the work and creates a thriving, productive, and happy workforce. We'll start by looking at some popular management theories from the past, spend some time conducting a pointed (and sometimes humorous) appraisal of the workplace of today, and start working on converting our thinking and actions to the Results-Only Work Environment (ROWE) management model and culture.

Throughout history, management theories have hovered around the idea that dispersing decision-making governance closer to the people will produce better results for the organization. For example, in 1911, Frederick Winslow creating "Taylorism," which argued that if managers treated employees as components that are replaceable, and directed work processes in a precise manner, both the employee and employer could prosper. The drawback was that people didn't behave as parts, gears or mechanisms. They behaved as people.

In 1923, Alfred P. Sloan took a much different approach—creating a bureaucracy that really was more decentralized and helped GM become the leading car and truck manufacturer worldwide. The idea was to delegate power to others—division leaders taking responsibility for revenue and profit expectations—rather than controlling the entire organization.

Other management theories were born out of the idea that understanding what actually motivates people is what will make businesses thrive. And, with that, the human relations movement was born. Workers may have become happier, but now were unfortunately subjected to silly team-building games.

One of my favorite popular management styles, "management by walking around" was introduced by Hewlett-Packard in the late 1930s. It's a style that's still used today. Managers are encouraged to wander around chatting with their employees. I guess this makes people feel noticed, but doesn't it also interrupt what they're trying to get done? It also creates a bit of paranoia. Why didn't my manager talk to me? Why does he always talk to Joe? Now he's taking Joe out to lunch! Of course Joe will get that next promotion. I suppose I'll need to take up golf.

This could be the beginnings of today's cultural staple, the one thing that keeps culture from evolving: the bitter, resentful, hostile language that screams "not fair, not fair" and keeps everyone focused on everything but the work.

In the 1950s, the idea was formed that top-down management should be abolished. Remember W. Edward Deming's quality management where the idea was that every person in a company should be focused on quality and not management-mandated sales quotas?

Wait a minute! This was 1950?

Deming became a cultural icon in Japan, where companies ferociously competed for the Deming Prize. By the mid-1980s, some American companies jumped in. Florida Power & Light Company became the first American company to go through the Deming process (which took several years and an investment of millions) and win the "American division" of the Deming Prize. Shortly after, the company appointed a new chief executive officer (CEO), who immediately dismantled the process at Florida Power & Light Company.

Right. Any program that doesn't become the DNA of the culture is sure to become a target for new leadership to abolish. And it creates a workplace of people who have a serious case of flavor-of-the-month fatigue. Another program? Ugh!

Does anyone out there truly believe that top-down management has been abolished? I actually think that it somehow became *more* top-down. But at least now we're all shouting, "The customer is king," even while we're arguing about who the customer really is, or if in fact everyone is the customer, or if we should create a cardboard cutout of the customer and place it on each floor of the organization. Just as a reminder, lest we forget.

I was personally swept up in the management craze of the 1990s, when the philosophy of servant leadership—created in the 1970s by former AT&T manager Robert Greenleaf—gained momentum. A servant leader shouldn't single-handedly pursue some higher goal; instead, they need to act as servants to their employees in an attempt to make them all happier.

I couldn't help but be perplexed as to how servant leadership was going to evolve as long as the still-thriving, top-down paternalistic system we call the "company" still existed. Daniel Pink, who published *Free Agent Nation: The Future of Working for Yourself* in 2001 argues that workers no longer need companies to employ them. He goes on to say:

> Legions of Americans, and increasingly citizens of other countries as well, are abandoning one of the Industrial Revolution's most enduring legacies—the "job"—and forging new ways to work. They're becoming self-employed knowledge workers, proprietors of home-based businesses, temps and permatemps, free-lancers and e-lancers, independent contractors and independent professionals, micropreneurs and infopreneurs, part-time consultants,

interim executives, on-call troubleshooters, and full-
time soloists. . . . They're swapping, or being forced
to swap, steady salaries for pay-for-performance
agreements that compensate them in commissions,
stock options, and bonuses.

And this new breed of worker isn't going away.
They're leading the fight for a new way to work and live.
In the meantime, we're scratching our heads trying to
figure out how to get them under control. We're trying
to figure out how to motivate them. Yet off they go
looking for something we can't quite put our fingers on.

In his 2009 book *Drive*, Pink lays out the shift from
extrinsic to intrinsic motivation. He states:

> The problem is that most businesses haven't caught
> up to this new understanding of what motivates
> us. Too many organizations—not just companies,
> but governments and nonprofits as well—still
> operate from assumptions about human potential
> and individual performance that are outdated,
> unexamined, and rooted more in folklore than in
> science. They continue to pursue practices such as
> short-term incentive plans and pay-for-perfor-
> mance schemes in the face of mounting evidence
> that such measures usually don't work and often
> do harm.

We get it. And we'd have to argue that a ROWE
is helping to drag us, kicking and screaming, into
the twenty-first century. It's taking us to a place where the
output of our work is what's important and where true
motivation doesn't come from an "on-campus coffee

shop" or a manager that continually interrupts us to ask "what did you do for fun over the weekend?"

"As leaders, we no longer need to worry about the 'how,'" says Keith Ryniak, the sales director for Wisconsin West for our client American Family Insurance. "Operating in a ROWE encourages our team to be intrinsically motivated to make their own 'how' to get the job done. Our management team has always focused on results and how to achieve them, but ROWE helps foster an environment of trust and confidence with our teams and their abilities to achieve those results."

Of course, *a lot* has happened since *Free Agent Nation* was published in 2001. The role of management has been theorized, reinvented, uninvented, challenged, elevated, loved, and hated—hence the view that "people don't leave *jobs;* they leave *managers.*"

Cali: How many times have you heard the saying, "People don't leave jobs; they leave managers"? Even though it's one of those things you hear year after year—that survey results reveal time and again—nothing ever changes. One of my biggest pet peeves (and Jody will attest to this!) is talking about the same things over and over and never getting anywhere. So please, *please* take the rest of this chapter seriously so that you can take some actions to help retain your employees, instead of having them continue to leave. Because in case you haven't heard, they're leaving you, not the company.

Okay. Our heads hurt. Does yours?

The root of the problem is that all this time, we've been trying to figure out how to manage the *people* to get the work done, instead of managing the *work* to get the work done. And this basic belief is what dictates that people first need to be managed—then the work. This is why we lose the chance to create a workforce dedicated to and motivated by achieving results—together.

In 2008, our client, Ryan, LLC, participated in on-site training to adopt a ROWE. In an article by Pete Fehrenbach in *SmartBusiness*, G. Brint Ryan, founder, CEO, and managing principal, began to see a ROWE pay off in a little more than a year:

> At the end of 2009, a miraculous thing happened. [We realized when] we looked at the metrics at the end of the year that we had done some remarkable things. First, we had reduced our turnover from 22.5 percent all the way down to 8 percent. We had to go back and recheck the numbers because we thought, wait—that can't be right.
>
> In addition, we posted the highest revenue we'd ever posted as a firm, *and* a record profit, in what was one of the absolute worst economic environments I've seen in my professional career. So we were beside ourselves.
>
> We're big believers in creating a work environment where people can do their best work, not one where we try to second-guess when they should come to work, or where they should work from. We know that people work differently. Some people like

to get up early in the morning and knock things out. Other people work later in the day, or they work at different times. And sometimes they're more effective when they're away from the office than when they're in the office.

Now let's talk about how *you* manage. Do you have office hours? Core hours? Policies around inclement weather or tardiness? Do you have dress codes, summer hours, and rules that govern vacations? If you can answer "yes" to any of these, then you are managing the people, not the work.

Let's start with office hours. Why do they even exist? Because almost everyone believes in the following equation:

$$\text{Time} + \text{physical presence} = \text{results}$$

We think that if people gather in the same physical space around the same time, work will somehow magically happen. We believe that it's best to build relationships face to face and that meetings are effective means of completing work. Work hours ensure that we are managing the people effectively and that work will get done as a result.

And, we must be professional, right? We establish dress code policies because we can't actually trust people to know how to dress. And if we don't make this abundantly clear, they might wear flip-flops and hot pants to a client meeting. If we don't have a dress code in place, people might dress in clothing that just doesn't support a "professional work environment." And we've all seen someone who really crossed the line (think beach clothes) with whom we had to have the embarrassing conversation to let that person know, "Hey, the office isn't the beach." It's easier to have a policy than to take care of a single case or two. Again, managing the people.

You get the point.

Curt Haats, chief financial officer of the Human Services and Public Health Department for Minnesota's Hennepin County in Minneapolis, puts it this way:

> There have been a lot of employee "empowerment" efforts throughout the years, and [we] at the senior management level have always tried to get employees engaged in working to improve our business. ROWE has by far been the most successful effort. Not only does it get the results message delivered throughout the organizations, [but] it actually has a method that [involves] everyone, at every level, in improving our business and creating more effective ways of doing things. And it does so without layers and layers of process and approvals.

Well said. But before we dive into how to manage the work and not the people, it's important to note that the way in which you manage the work is the same for everyone. That is, it has nothing to do with any differences in attitudes, perceptions, and behaviors. It's not about accommodation, gender, ethnicity, generation, or the like. Everyone has the same goal: the work. And focusing on this levels the playing field. Everyone is hired to produce results, and for a manager, this is golden.

> Cali: I often hear from organizations interested in a
> ROWE that they like how the foundation levels
> everything out. In fact, we hear from diversity folks
> a lot; they are happy to see that there is finally a
> workplace strategy that will pave the way for inclu-
> sion efforts to thrive. A ROWE makes sure that
> anyone can enter, and stay part of, the organiza-
> tion—as long as he or she delivers results.

No more subjective conversations ridden with lame
excuses about why someone missed a deadline. No more
laborious weeks trying to figure out who's in and who's
out. No more sleepless nights wondering if everyone
knows what they're supposed to be doing. No more
worry in the pit of your stomach that you feel you have to
do it yourself to get it done right. You can create an
organization where everyone can achieve his or her
highest potential, regardless of packaging.

"A clear benefit of a ROWE is the quality of
work that is done," says Learner's Edge owner Kyle
Pederson. He goes on to say:

> The service we provide is largely a creative one
> (designing and developing continuing education
> courses for teachers). As with any type of creative
> work, the artist (or curriculum writer, in our case)
> can't simply flip a switch and churn out his or her best
> work. You need to be in "the zone." And it's hard, if

not impossible, to get into that zone on any given day between the hours of 8 and 5 while sitting at your office desk. In a ROWE, our course creators have the ability to work where and when they do their best, most creative work. For some that's at home; for some it's the coffee shop; for some it actually *is* squirreled away in their offices. And that's what a ROWE encourages. And because of that, we're producing (on the whole) more creative, engaging, and well-written courses. I think the same "quality bump" happens for other products/services we offer as well. Our staff can write reports, return e-mails, and network with potential clients and partners during those hours/locations when they are on top of their game. They no longer need to slog through an unproductive 8–11 AM shift where they stumble over their words and need three cups of coffee to be functional, only to craft a document that fails to impress or inspire.

Sounds pretty fantastic, doesn't it? But we have to sacrifice one more sacred cow in order to get there, the one artificial construct that essentially defines current management philosophy. This theory shapes not only the way you manage performance, but more than likely, the way you think about work. And that, of course, is our specific, measurable, achievable, relevant, timely goals—that is, our S.M.A.R.T. goals.[1]

---

[1] Yes, there are several definitions of S.M.A.R.T., but this is most commonly used.

Cali: Have to pop in again about these good ol' S.M.A.R.T. goals! It makes me shudder thinking of how much time and energy organizations spent training countless employees on how to write S.M.A.R.T. goals in a non-ROWE. When we were employees at Best Buy we had goals experts and human resources (HR) trying to teach us; we had guidebooks and worksheets. But in the end, no one cared. We all knew it didn't matter if goals were accomplished or not; the same people would be rewarded for coming in early, leaving late, and working weekends. "Oh, Tim didn't reach his S.M.A.R.T. goal last quarter? He put in a lot of effort, though, so good for him!" We knew the game. All you had to do was come up with some S.M.A.R.T. goals that would pass (meaning the measurable and timely parts might not be too strong) but complain about how many hours you worked, and it would be all good.

When you think of the time you spend producing these goals, performing reviews, and providing documentation to HR, don't you wish you had some of that time back to manage the work? Let's expose how useless this methodology is for defining and measuring the work. It's not that S.M.A.R.T. goals—or other suspiciously similar goal-setting processes with fun acronyms are bad; it's just that there is a major component missing: everyone being crystal clear about the outcome.

If I said, "Everyone meet me at 9:00 AM tomorrow morning; we're going on a vacation!" what would your first question be? It's obvious: you need to know where we're going so you can perform the activities necessary and pack the right clothing and supplies to prepare for a successful vacation. Or do you?

Let's get ready for the "vacation" using the S.M.A.R.T. goals framework. Imagine you're in the logistics department, and we create a S.M.A.R.T. goal around "packing for vacation":

Specific: I will pack (shorts, T-shirts, swimsuit, sunscreen, and flip-flops).

Measurable: I will pack in a 24-inch suitcase, keeping the weight to less than 50 pounds.

Achievable: I have the means and ability to accomplish this task.

Relevant: We're going on a trip, so this is an important activity: packing.

Timely: I will have my task completed by 10 PM tonight so that I'm ready for action!

Now you believe you've successfully achieved your S.M.A.R.T. goal—that is, if Hawaii is the destination or outcome. But you haven't because we're going to Vail, Colorado, to snowboard. You've packed the wrong things! Now your performance in Vail is subpar. You're busy running around shopping for warm clothes, snowboard equipment, and the like. You've also wasted a whole suitcase on beach clothes, so you now have to buy another suitcase to carry your new purchases home. Now you're wasting time *and* resources.

What's the point of this? Even though you established a "reasonable" set of S.M.A.R.T. goals—that were even aligned with the outcome of vacation—they weren't crystal clear about the outcome. Leaving out one small piece—the destination—resulted in getting to the wrong outcome. Nevertheless, you worked just as hard and met every one of your S.M.A.R.T. goals!

Wow. Now just imagine this happening all over your organization. Say 10, 100, 500, or 5,000 people on teams doing lots of activities (working hard!) that may or may not be heading in the right direction. But they've achieved their S.M.A.R.T. goals. Check!

We'd like to introduce a different framework here— one that's working and one that gets everyone aligned first. This way, creating measurable results is effective and achievable. This framework is outcome-based thinking, and it generates an environment where performance is managed on a continual basis. That means all the time, not just at the yearly performance review meeting.

"Ideas for profitable growth began to be daily conversations around the office," says Jeffrey Buchanan, founder and CEO of JL Buchanan, a Minneapolis-based retail consulting company. In addition,

> People at all levels were formulating plans for business growth and collaborating with each other on how to bring those ideas to life. Our growth came from a variety of directions, because we had a variety of people thinking about it. Discovering and

developing new clients, new services, new products, new ideas, and new approaches have become a part of our everyday thinking. Our business has grown 80 percent since we went through ROWE training in 2009. We have added many new services to our portfolio and created 15 new positions in our company. Our profit is healthy, and we have created a reward program for achieving our results. The reward is a perk, but really, reaching the goal together is also a huge point of pride for our team. We are accomplishing great things together where *everyone* contributes *every day*.

Exactly. ROWE-trained organizations thrive by continually examining the five questions that everyone needs to be able to answer to be part of a dynamic results-focused organization:

1. What is the ultimate outcome?
2. Who is the ultimate customer?
3. What are we doing that is enabling the ultimate outcome?
4. What are we doing that's not?
5. How will we measure success?

Ask yourself, "Does everyone on my team or in my organization know what ultimate outcome we're trying to achieve?" You probably won't find it in the vision or mission statement, which shouldn't come as a surprise, because that's what the people at the top handed down.

Try this little exercise, and you'll see what I mean. Simply ask your team, "What is our ultimate outcome as an organization? Why do we exist?" Have each person write down what he or she thinks it is on a piece of paper. Some will struggle to regurgitate the mission and others might remember the vision. All of the answers will likely be different, maybe extremely or slightly so, but they certainly won't be 100 percent spot on. And therein lies the first problem: the outcome simply isn't a part of your employees' DNA. It's not what makes people wake up in the morning raring to go.

Even though they don't hold the precise answers, the mission and vision are good places to start. They'll prompt your people to determine a broader outcome, one that they can own and feel excited about and that drives the right activities and gets them thinking creatively. It's a response they can give when someone at a cocktail party asks, "So, what do you do?"

Most people answer this question by mindlessly reciting their job title. People are attached to it and feel that it shows their status (or lack thereof). It's something to which people can say, "Wow, nice job, buddy" or "Oh. Entry level, eh?" And imagine if someone rattled off his organization's 50-word mission statement when asked this question. People would think he was a little crazy (unless, of course, he owned the company).

So put your mission or vision statement up in front of everyone and ask, "So what? If we do this, then what?" Tell them that they will be using whatever they come up with when asked, "What do you do?" in the future. It will be simple and compelling and will make you proud to say it.

Here's an example. Say your mission statement is: "It is the mission of ABC Car Gadgets to provide car owners with the right products and knowledge that fulfill their wants and needs every time. We strive each day to enrich lives with customer-driven value." That's a great statement, and if true, the customer will be happy and the company will make money. However, it's quite a mouthful and not something you can easily spew out or rally around. Who gets up in the morning and thinks, "Today I'm going to provide car owners with the right products and knowledge that fulfills their wants and needs every time . . . Hooray!"? And who would ever give that answer at a cocktail party?

It must be real for the people, not just a fancy statement on the website or in the annual report. Ask your people, "If we actually do what the mission states, then what?" You might get:

"Customers will be happy, because they'll have what they need to go places."

"The cars will work, so people can get around."

"We help people go places."

"I help people go places."

Bingo!

Now let's go back to the cocktail party. Imagine if everyone in your organization—from the receptionist, to the parts supervisor, to the accounts receivable clerk, to the communications specialist, to the information technology (IT) manager—answered the question, "What do you do?" with "I help people go places." Then the conversation can go in a whole new direction. You'll see your people start to gel as a team, connecting what they do to everyone else.

"You help people go places?"

"Yes, I work for ABC Car Gadgets. I make sure every customer who visits our store has a great experience by making sure that person gets what's needed the first time. No returns."

This is not about a job title. It's about being part of a team of people, with all members knowing that they are just as important as the next guy. It's about making it clear to your people that no job or title is less important than another—and that every single person feels accountable to the broader outcome.

If the person at ABC Car Gagets doesn't create a great experience for the customer when working—and ensure that the person got what was needed the first time—then that worker didn't help people go places. That person helped people get frustrated, slowed down the "going places" piece, and affected the bottom line. That worker might have even lost a customer.

WATT Publishing, Compnay's Tara Leitner, whose team completed ROWE training with CultureRx in the summer of 2012, had this to say:

> As a manager, it's imperative that your team understand the company's outcome first and then how departments and individuals fit into that outcome. If they don't, they remain task-oriented, which means that you aren't getting the best part of

[the employees]—their original thoughts, their creativity, the ideas that move your company forward. Some employees may need more coaching in this area (hey managers, that's your job!), and once they get it, they might just be the ones with the most ideas. These are the employees who've been too busy doing and being annoyed by unnecessary tasks. In that environment, "being innovative" wasn't even a passing thought; it was a daunting hindrance. Now that we have a clearly established outcome, employees are actively making decisions themselves, saving everyone time and yielding better results overall. An action-oriented employee who knows the outcome and feels in control of it is also more responsible, creative, and engaged. My team now readily comes to me with ideas for process improvements, new products, and solutions to challenges.

Outcome-based thinking isn't a new idea. But because the mission or vision statement has been handed down from above, posterized, put on a wall, and printed in the company handbook, it's simply not easily remembered. It's not exciting. It's not *mine*.

So avoid putting the new rallying cry on the website, T-shirts, mugs, pens, security badges, or office walls. Once you do that, it now belongs to the organization, not the people. The rallying cry can align with the mission and vision; the people just have to own it.

Once people are supporting the broader outcome—one they remember, that excites them—it's time to figure out who the ultimate customer is. And there is only one.

Often, you will hear people say, "Everyone is my customer" or "I have internal and external customers." When everyone in your organization is serving 14 different customers, the real customer becomes lost.

Think of everyone who's not the ultimate customer as a resource or tool that you can use to serve the ultimate customer. For example, let's say that you're in the public relations department for a particular company. You may say that the *Wall Street Journal, Time* magazine, or a particular journalist is your customer. But none of these in are. They're resources that you use to communicate to your ultimate customer—perhaps about your organization's new product or efforts to "go green." In either case, you're talking to the customer, and that's not a journalist.

So who is your ultimate customer? Everyone in the organization must agree on who this is so that employees direct all work activities toward delighting the one customer.

ABC Car Gadgets' customer is the shopper who buys parts and services, whether in the physical stores or via the website. Some might say, "Well that's easy for store clerks to figure out. They come in direct contact with the customer every day. I'm in corporate human resources and spend my time serving what I thought were my corporate clients in the office every day. How do I affect the 'ultimate customer'?"

This is what every person in every position of every department needs to figure out and connect to. Otherwise, your work activities might fit nicely into your S.M.A.R.T. goal, but for the most part, they're irrelevant.

The human resources employee is responsible for corporate culture, retaining and attracting talent, management coaching, and the like. If human resource professionals do *their* job well, then the resources (employees) have the right foundation to do their jobs well; this, in turn, filters down to the ultimate customer. If they don't do their jobs well, then engagement, morale, and productivity suffer, in turn affecting—you guessed it—the ultimate customer.

"Taking our staff through ROWE training certainly helped them understand that their work environment was changing. [It allowed us to express] that their job wasn't to show up in an office from 8:00 AM and leave at 4:30 PM; rather, it was to deliver services to our customers in need—to get the best results whenever and wherever they could," says Haats, CFO of The Human Services and Public Health Department of Hennepin County, Minnesota. "However, an added benefit to us was that all levels of the organization recognized that we, management, actually want their input in deciding how best to get the results the organization wants."

So it's imperative that each person figure out what he or she does on a daily basis that enables the ultimate outcome and, in turn, serves the customer. It's equally crucial for all employees to figure out what they do that doesn't contribute to this at all. You'll mostly discover that there is a lot of wasted time—really, a lot.

We talked about the concept of *presenteeism* in *Why Work Sucks and How to Fix It*. This is simply what occurs when you're in the office but are unproductive or not working for whatever reason. Presenteeism accounts for 80 percent of lost productivity in the workplace.

Here are a few things that waste time:

1. Attending status update meetings where everyone on a project takes turns talking about his or her piece (Hey, we can read. And if we have a question, we can ask.)

2. Sitting in traffic when you could be working

3. Counting or tracking hours

4. Trying to meet minimum or maximum hours guidelines

5. Fielding constant interruptions because you have to be in the office

6. Meeting core hours requirements

7. Wasting time in unproductive, brainstorming, or unplanned meetings (We'll tackle meetings in Chapter 5.)

8. Dealing with people who aren't clear about when they need something ("I need that by Tuesday at 3 PM" is clear; "I'd like that ASAP" is not.)

9. Engaging in "forced fun" team-building events (I'd rather spend time with my family/friends outside of work.)

10. Working with people who aren't held accountable for their work and who end up slowing down the process for everyone else

Depending on the work, all employees will have a sense of where—and on what—they're wasting time. And by letting each person take ownership of his or her time—*and* the authority to remove wasted time from work—you essentially allow each person more time for what matters. If all I'm doing every day is filling my time to fit into office hours, I'm more apt to fill it with any activities just to keep from going insane.

"One clear benefit of a ROWE has been improved customer service," says Pederson, owner of Learner's Edge. "Our staff no longer conceives of work as something that happens only between the hours of 8 AM and 5 PM Monday through Friday. Much of our staff likes working in the evenings and occasionally on the weekends—so our customer is finding e-mails and calls returned (and live chats available) more immediately than pre-ROWE. It would be hard to overstate the impact that this 'customer service availability' has on our [current] or potential customer."

Okay. Now that everyone agrees with the ultimate outcome—customer—as well as with which activities are enabling the ultimate outcome and which are not, it's time for measurement.

Measures have to be clear and specific, and most important, they must prove that the activity being performed is relevant and defendable against the ultimate outcome and customer.

The following are two examples of how organizations with which we have worked have used the five-question method—instead of a more typical policy-driven or S.M.A.R.T. goal—to drive performance.

Example 1

- **POLICY-DRIVEN/S.M.A.R.T. GOAL:** To remain cohesive as a team, everyone needs to be in the office Tuesday, Wednesday, and Thursday between 9 AM and 3 PM **(S, M, A, T)**. Anyone who needs to be out of the office during these times must get permission **(S, T)** so that customer needs don't suffer. *(The R goal definitely seems to be missing here, and if it's not relevant, it's not important.)*

- **PERFORMANCE-DRIVEN GOAL:** Expanding perceived hours of operation will help us *make life fun and easy* **(outcome)** for our guests **(the customers)** by meeting them where they are. Therefore, starting September 1, we will make e-mail support available 24/7 **(result)**. We will track sales and customer satisfaction metrics **(measures)**, working with the retail support team to further refine measures that target the success of this change for 90 days and then reevaluate.

Example 2

- **POLICY-DRIVEN/S.M.A.R.T. GOAL:** When you're working off-site, I'll need to see a log of activities you are completing each hour during an 8-hour period **(S, M)**. You need to submit this at the end of each day **(T, M)** that you are working off-site **(A)**. (Again, is this **R**elevant?)

- **PERFORMANCE-DRIVEN GOAL:** Conquering the backlog of applications will ensure that the citizens of XYZ County **(our customer)** who require these services are living in a safe and healthy manner **(outcome)**. Therefore, we are going to process applications wherever makes the most sense to get them completed at the time service is required **(result)**. We will measure call volume, application process time, and window wait time **(measures)** to make sure we effectively and efficiently meet our outcome.

The S.M.A.R.T. goal methodology is sound. However, it's often not effective in practice if it's being used to drive policy—or when the people writing the goals are not clear about the outcome they are driving toward or the customer they are serving. It's also not effective if old-fashioned, irrelevant workplace policies are more important than the work.

Setting, reviewing, and documenting S.M.A.R.T. goals are the last things that desperate managers do on the last Friday before they are due, whereas outcome-based goals are ongoing, team-driven, and always relevant.

It's not easy at first to adopt the outcome-based method to manage performance. But the hard work that takes place during the first few months pays off in spades as people continually challenge what's relevant and what's not. Conversations become more focused—objective, not subjective—as people begin to plan more effectively.

The following is a simple example of a subjective versus an objective performance conversation.

Subjective (Manager Approaches Employee)

Manager: Nancy, I see you've been missing some deadlines lately.

Nancy: I know. It's hard to keep up.

Manager: Is your daughter home on the days you're teleworking? I know how hard it must be trying to take care of her *and* do work at the same time.

Nancy: She is home one of the days.
Manager: You may need to put her in day care that day.
Nancy: Perhaps.
Manager: Another option is to come into the office every day. That might help you focus.

Now, let's take that pointless conversation and make it about what matters. In a ROWE, managers are not chasing employees around. Employees are keeping management apprised of issues as they arise.

Objective (Employee Approaches Manager)

Nancy: I want to make you aware of a couple of deadlines that are at risk.
Manager: Great. Tell me what's going on.
Nancy: I've been working with the vendor relations team to ensure product delivery to the stores is on track. They are experiencing issues with supply, and it's putting the visual display team's timeline at risk as well in the Southwest region.
Manager: Where do you think I can best help you?
Nancy: I would like you to escalate this issue to the director.
Manager: I will do that today and get back to you by 4 PM. From there we will decide how to approach this.
Nancy: Great. I'll inform the team.

Organizations that have trained with CultureRx to become a ROWE evolve into an outcome-based, performance-driven culture. Discussions like the one mentioned here are just the way the business operates.

"A good way to compare how management approaches the work differently now that we're in a ROWE is to take a look at the kinds of questions/comments we posted before and how we approach them today," says Pederson of Learner's Edge. He continues:

"Before we would say things like:

- "I'm not sure Sally can handle any more work . . . she seems to be pretty busy around here. She arrives pretty early and doesn't take long lunch breaks."
- "Sally was late with that project? Well, probably understandable. We must have overloaded her a bit. She hasn't taken much paid time off lately."
- "Is there a deadline? Well, Sally, that's a good question. We'd certainly like things to be done by August 1, but we know you're doing lots of things, so basically keep plugging away while you're here. Hopefully you'll be able to hit the deadline."
- "Is Ricky late *again?* Just bothers me how he doesn't set a good work ethic for everybody else. People need to be accountable for their time and we need to have consistent expectations of everybody."

Now that we're a ROWE, we focus on what matters, so we sound like this:

- "Sally, this is a project that needs to be completed by August 1."
- "Sally, you didn't have the project done by August 1. I know before a ROWE, deadlines were merely

suggestions. But in a ROWE, deadlines are important. If you think we've set one unreasonably, you need to let me know well in advance of that deadline. Otherwise, I'm confident that you are managing your projects, work, and time so that you can meet deadlines precisely when we need."

• "It doesn't matter if Ricky is here, there, or anywhere else right now. What matters is that he gets his work done and meets his results against our defined outcome."

At this point you might still have lingering questions about how you can *really* manage people this way. But know that with each incremental step you take and each tip or trick you decide to try, you'll get closer to managing *work,* rather than *people,* in a way that makes sense for the twenty-first century.

Typical Questions

The following are typical questions managers ask when they're thinking about a ROWE for their team or organization. These questions are important because evolving to a ROWE requires a different way of solving common challenges. Lose no sleep! Here are the answers.

Q: What if someone misses a deadline?

A: A deadline is part of "getting the work done"; it's not a suggestion. People seem to have a lot of excuses for missing deadlines today. "Bob didn't do his part, so I couldn't do mine," "I wasn't sure if the deadline was set in stone," or even "I have too much on my plate." If a deadline is at risk, then it's the employee's responsibility to communicate that to the manager. *Each employee is accountable* for the work. If he or she cannot—or does not—let the manager know about this, then perhaps that person needs to work somewhere else.

Q: How will I know the work is getting done?

A: This is the best part. If you've done the hard work with everyone to establish the correct measures, you know exactly what work everyone has agreed to accomplish. Then, you can use everyone's input to establish how you as a manager will *see them getting work done*—and whatever this is depends on what you and your team decide. Perhaps they'll submit progress reports on an internal shared drive or cloud-based application. Maybe you'll have more frequent performance discussions and check in with your employees on how the work is progressing. But you will not be "managing by (physically) walking around."

Q: What if another person's failure to do his or her job affects my outcome?

A: If communicating exactly what you need, and when you need it by to the person who is negatively affecting the outcome doesn't produce action, then you must escalate the issue to the manager, who then needs to take immediate action. It's not personal. It's business.

Q: How do you fire someone in a ROWE?

A: We constantly hear from companies that use traditional structures that it's almost impossible to fire someone. That's because people can look like they're working, show up and put in time, and continue to say they'll try harder. That's crap. In a ROWE, everyone is clear about what he or she needs to accomplish and how it will be measured. Performance discussions are *objective*, not subjective. As a manager, you can easily see nonperformance, document it, and take a nonperformer quickly through the steps (verbal warning, written warning, *out*) to exit that person from your organization. Remember, you're paying *adults* to do what they have agreed to do; it's not personal.

Q: What about new hires who come into a ROWE culture? How will they get trained if people aren't around?

A: First, new hires—just like everyone else getting a paycheck—need to start out from day one with clear direction on what they were hired to do, and how their progress will be measured. This is an objective conversation between the manager and new hire. A ROWE is not a traditional flexible workplace, so it does operate differently; nobody's judging how other people are spending their time (Sludge), and the language is entirely results-focused. People are treated like, and act like adults. Nobody's asking permission to come in late or leave early. Everyone has complete autonomy. Some of our larger clients have a ROWE training for new hires to give them foundational knowledge of the culture (including reading *Why Work Sucks and How to Fix It*). Smaller organizations have less formal indoctrinations. And the question about 'nobody being around'? This is the twenty-first century. We have voice mail and e-mail. If we require a face to face interaction, we can negotiate that instead of wandering around looking for people like in the olden days.

Things to Try

1. Meet with your team and align on the ultimate outcome of your organization.

2. Agree on what activities constitute wasted time and stop doing them.

3. Review and remove all ambiguous language from your goals and replace it with concrete measurable goals statements. ("Optimize" is ambiguous. "Increase by 20 percent" is a clear measure.)

4. Review and remove any subjective language from your goals that you are not measuring in a specific manner and that smack of "I don't trust you," such as, "Be recognized as a team player."

5. Review timelines and deadlines for any goals you feel are at risk. Make it clear that deadlines are not *suggestions*. Seek agreement with those responsible for anything at risk to make sure deadlines will be achieved.

(continued)

(continued)

Things to Avoid

1. Engaging in subjective performance discussions. It doesn't matter if someone is working from home with a toddler in tow; the work still needs to get done. Period. Talk about the *work*.

2. Creating new policies and guidelines that lock workers into fixed processes, rules, or schedules that do not allow them to use common sense to manage work and personal pursuits.

3. Assuming that expectations are clear. If you're nervous about whether people are putting in 40 hours, then expectations aren't clear and *measurable*.

4. Dictating how people will "team up" to get work done. Just because you like everyone in a room on a whiteboard doesn't mean that's the most effective method.

5. Calling every Tom, Dick, and Harry your customer. You have one. Who is it?

Get Support!

1. Schedule a Workshop for your team and get aligned once and for all. Learn more by visiting www.gorowe.com/training.

2. Download your copy of the e-book Building a Performance-Based Work Culture by visiting www.gorowe.com/books-and-tools.

Down with Billable Hours, Up with Results

by Otmara "Omi" Diaz-Cooper and Todd Cooper

Otmara "Omi" Diaz-Cooper and Todd Cooper are the president and vice president/creative director, of Diaz & Cooper, a Miami-based Web development and digital marketing agency. They completed CultureRx's on-site ROWE training in March 2012.

It was the end of another billing cycle, and once again, our invoices were late going out the door. The reason was that many creative team members had not yet turned in their time sheets—and who could blame them? Time sheets are tedious, are boring, and take away from time they could be spending to produce and think creatively. Those who waited until the end of the week to do their time sheets often had to "guesstimate"—and worse yet, the time limits cut into creativity and strategic thinking. Meanwhile, accounting personnel had to sit on their hands until they received the time sheets to be able to generate invoices.

The culture of estimating, keeping track of, billing by, and worrying about not having enough *time* to count the time is so prevalent that it's practically dogma in the advertising industry. We struggled with this model for years, trying different ways to keep time. We used manual sheets and little desktop timers until finally we discovered an online software system that made it pretty easy to track

(continued)

(*continued*)

time and connect it to billing. But right when we got really good at tracking time for every employee on every project, we realized the futility of this model.

The situation goes like this: Ad agencies track what they produce by the time they spend on projects; these are known as billable hours. By getting paid for hours worked, they earn their money on execution, which is actually what clients value the least. Execution is a commodity, and there is always someone around the corner (not to mention across the ocean) who can do it for a few dollars less per hour. Essentially, it's a race to the bottom. A client will never say, "You must have done a really good job solving my problem, because you spent a ton of time and I just received a huge bill from you!"

What clients *really* value—what they hire and keep agencies for—is critical thinking, creativity, innovation, and, most important, the results that spring from the agency's ideas.

The most potent realization we came to is that the billable hour model causes a vast misalignment of goals between the client and the agency. If an agency is incredibly efficient and completes a project very quickly, the client benefits because the project will cost less, regardless of the value produced. On the other hand, if an agency is *in*efficient and takes a lot of hours and manpower to produce the same project, the client suffers from overpaying, but the agency gets to charge a lot more. Not only is the billable hour model counterproductive, but it's also self-limiting. There is a ceiling on earning when one charges based only on number of hours times number of employees. This production mentality and the 40-hour workweek made sense for Industrial Age factory workers and day laborers; however, it's pretty much obsolete for today's professional firms. After all, we are in a knowledge-based industry, hired to create marketing solutions that make our clients more money.

Once we realized how this model didn't serve either our clients or ourselves, we changed our pricing structure to fixed fees that were based on a project's value, a concept known as *value pricing*. This shifted our focus away from tracking hours and on to achieving results through our marketing solutions. It was a very freeing move that now allows us to spend as much, or as little, time as it takes to solve a particular problem without the frustration of having to "watch the clock." By concentrating on producing results, we are able to mutually align the client's and agency's interests.

So what does all this have to do with a Results-Only Work Environment (ROWE)? We figured that now that we as an agency are holding ourselves accountable for results for our clients, why not bring that same model internally and hold our team members accountable for *their* results only? Not results as the hours they log on a time sheet, but the

(continued)

(*continued*)

quality of their critical thinking and the benefit of the solutions they bring to the table. Think about it: as value pricing aligns our financial interests with our clients', so does ROWE align our values with our workforce's. Developers can spend time figuring out new deployment methods; accounting is free to bill on time and then go home to run an errand; and the creative types are more productive—everyone can focus on solutions instead of time. After all, what does it really matter to our clients if inspiration struck 1 hour or 20 hours into a project, as long as we are producing the desired results? Today, we at Diaz & Cooper are all measured by the same performance metrics: the results we produce and the value we create.

The concept of a "distributed" workforce is already fairly common among Web development companies, and although it has some similarities to a ROWE, we knew that the absolute, total focus on producing results as our ultimate outcome was the perfect internal counterpoint to our customer-facing philosophy of pricing our work based on business goals (key performance indicators [KPIs]) achieved for our clients. This concept also feeds directly into our mission to "transform business into a playground of opportunity and become indispensable through innovation, value, and results."

The ROWE model has indeed made us more effective. Our teams are more collaborative, our meetings are more succinct, and people are asking more thoughtful questions. We've actually grown closer as a team, even though we are not always in the office together. ROWE has given us a cultural advantage over other agencies, especially when it comes to recruiting great talent and retaining an A-team. It's pretty hard to compete with the idea of being chief executive officer of your own time and life. Our people are jazzed about work, some for the first time in a long while. Now that our team members have control of their own time, they are coming up with ways to make their work more meaningful by bringing new ideas and energy to the organization. All of this adds to the firm creating a more enriching experience for employees, which in turn has had a direct positive impact on the *value* our agency brings to clients.

4

24/7 Kicks 9–5's Ass

I f you're going to have a team that functions well together, everyone has to communicate effectively. It's a word that we throw around a lot, right? *Communicate* is defined as "to express oneself in such a way that one is readily and clearly understood." And these days, we have a plethora of tools that enable us to communicate anytime and from anywhere. But despite all the wonderful things this lets us do, it's this "always-on" mentality that can cause people to feel overwhelmed and never able to "unplug." The people in organizations with which we work express this need to unplug as one of their biggest challenges. Many aren't sure how to manage the flow of communication bombarding them while still maintaining some semblance of a life.

We'll tackle that very challenge in this chapter.

Keeping traditional office hours is one method people use to manage the flow of information. This approach says that you can stop working when you leave the office. You have an acceptable reason for leaving those pesky e-mails and voice mails until the next business day. Even if an emergency was to present itself, you could tap into the golden nugget of excuses: "I always unplug after hours. I cherish this time with my family." Okay. That's understandable.

However, this widely held belief that work has—and *should have*—a certain beginning and end point not only bogs down the flow of communication but causes us to do things we wouldn't normally do to keep the wolves (the organization) from taking over our lives. You saw this in Chapter 2 when Cali clearly described how, as managers, we think it's our job to protect people's off hours even when unknowingly sabotaging that ourselves by saying things like, "Let's give it up for Jill! She gave up time with her family to take care of that customer issue."

"In 2009, we set out to double our business by the end of 2014. We needed a tool to help us communicate and motivate the entire JL Buchanan team to embrace change, think differently, and engage in the mission," says Susan Hoaby, president of JL Buchanan, a Minneapolis-based retail consulting company. She adds,

When we launched [a Results-Only Work Environment (ROWE)] with CultureRx in May of that year with a team of 22 employees, we laid out the long-term objective and, together, established the short-term objectives to deliver. Our message was simple and clear: we wanted everyone to concentrate on driving smart and healthy growth for the organization that would allow us to navigate the [current] economic shifts and thrive in the future. We didn't tell everyone specifically what to do, or how to accomplish the goal; we simply made clear the results we wanted to achieve.

The first year of our journey was exciting and challenging. Everyone was thrilled to have the ability to work where and when they wanted. We didn't really understand how important increasing our communication and being clear about our expectations of each other would be.

Communication, coupled with its sister theme, collaboration, is a topic mired in many deeply held beliefs. Study after study has proved beyond the shadow of a doubt that the best way to communicate is face to face. Yet people often don't have the option, especially when interacting globally, to communicate face to face with people they *haven't* met or may never "meet" in a traditional sense. The difference is that they don't have the luxury of hanging on to tired-old beliefs that are backed up by mountains of research. They have a common platform: the work. So they build a relationship around *that*.

But still we hang on to old communication styles with fondness. Remember the two cans with a string attached? Party lines? *Dialing* the telephone? How about the busy signal? Oh, and let's not forget "while you were out" pink slips! These might seem like relics of the past; however, we *still* behave in many ways like we're back in the good ol' days. After all, isn't it better to communicate by yelling across the cubicles to a coworker (aka, two cans and a string)? How about calling someone incessantly but refusing to leave a voice mail because you want that person to answer (busy signal)? Even better, leaving a note on someone's office chair, which the person might not see for days because he or she is not coming into the physical office ("while you were out pink slip")! And I love how people listen in on coworkers' conversations and jump in with their unsolicited two cents (party lines).

We get it. You want to insulate yourself from the bombardment of communication. And, you don't want to be available 24/7.

But unfortunately, you already are.

The second we all got answering machines, we suddenly became "available" 24/7. Of course, you did have the ability back then to ceremoniously unplug your answering machine from time to time. Today, we have the modern version of the answering machine, voice mail, which we can't unplug. Anyone can access you right now, 24/7, 365 days a year by leaving you a voice mail.

Let's take this a step further, because now, you don't just have an office phone and a home phone. You have an office phone with voice mail, a home phone with voice mail, and a mobile phone with voice mail (or maybe even two—one for business and one personal). Your mobile phone can even send text messages.

And then there's e-mail, not to mention instant messaging.

Communication is coming at you from all directions.

Back in the olden days, we were comforted by the fact that we could effectively shut off communication. At least we had only one phone with one answering machine. Today, we're bombarded with it. And we need to get a grip.

The first step is to accept the fact that despite what you believe (or want to believe), you are *already available* 24/7, 365 days a year. You may not be physically available, but your alter egos, voice mail and e-mail, are. At any time, day or night, these superheroes are standing in as the virtual *you*. You're sleeping? No problem. Voice mail has it. You're in the bathroom? No worries. E-mail's got you covered. On a call with a client? Yup. Voice mail's on it.

Of course, knowing that you have alter egos to store communication for you is a good thing. First, you can now *respond* to your messages when you're (1) out of the bathroom, (2) done with a meeting, or (3) whenever. You can *respond* to the need of the person who has reached out to you. You are not unavailable. You are willing, able, and poised to *respond*.

Now *you* are in control.

Getting work done and satisfying customer needs is not about *availability*. It's about *responding* to the need.

Ronnie Wooten is the president and chief operations officer of Financial Institution Technologies d/b/a Suntell, a Topeka-based organization with a focus on delivering integrated commercial loan risk management software solutions to the banking industry. Wooten recounts transitioning her company to a ROWE:

> One of the biggest management mind-set shifts I had to make after transitioning to a ROWE was

[knowing] that I could not expect an immediate response from anyone on the team. I was accustomed to shooting off an e-mail and getting a response within seconds. Granted, pre-ROWE training with CultureRx, I was sitting in an office within 4 feet of the staff—and I'd send out an e-mail rather than walk out and talk to them. BOOM! Immediate response. I couldn't see anyone post-ROWE, since 95 percent of us chose to meet results from a location other than the corporate office. I'd send an e-mail . . . and wait. And wait. And wait. After 2 minutes had passed and I hadn't received a response, the old-school manager mind-set would kick in. Where are they? What are they doing? Isn't anyone in this company working? I had to train myself to send the e-mail and walk away and trust the person *would* respond. And lo and behold, *they did!* And I received the answer I needed in a time frame that was perfectly acceptable. It wasn't within 2 seconds, but it was reasonable and acceptable. And no one suffered because the response wasn't instantaneous.

Are we paranoid? No. A recent study published by the MIT Sloan Management Review underscored the importance of being seen by one's boss as available at all times. They call this passive face time. Passive face time requires merely being seen in the workplace; to be credited with it, you need your manager only to observe you at work. It doesn't matter what you're doing or how well you're doing it. In a nutshell, your boss expects you to be available should something come up. So even if you're basically checked out, you need to give the *impression* of being on high alert.

No wonder we're all losing our minds. Being available was important to work in the Industrial Age. Today, in the twenty-first century, we have the technology and tools we need to *respond*. And we will.

Unfortunately, we can undermine ourselves—and the customer—simply by the way in which we use voice mail and e-mail. How we use these methods to communicate with one another is making us our own worst enemy. And, it's focused inward, not outward. It's about us and our perceived self-preservation—or as the authors of the MIT Sloan Management Review like to refer to it, perception management—not about the customer.

Cali: This is one of the big issues we run into in agency work culture. The biggest concern is, "What about our clients? They expect us to be available *all* the time. If they call, we need to answer. If they drop by, we need to be at our desks. If they sneeze, we need to wipe their noses." This is the area where we help clients gently retrain their customers/clients. Just because you bring your phone to the restroom with you or stick yourself to a chair for 10 straight hours doesn't mean your clients are getting what they need. Clarification: what they *really* need. Once clients can see that they'll get even *better* service when you focus on results instead of pleasing them through meaningless physical presence and extinguishing the rest of your life, you'll be in good shape. However, it takes deliberate effort by a group of people, supported by "the top" to move into this client retraining.

Let's look at a typical outgoing voice mail message from the customer perspective.

"Hi, this is Bill. It's Monday, February 11. I'll be in meetings most of the day. I'm unavailable to take your call right now (or I'm not at my desk right now). Please leave a message, and I'll call you as soon as possible."

Let's dissect this piece by piece.

"Hi, this is Bill." Good. It's good to know I called the right person. This is spot on!

"It's Monday, February 11." Thank you, but I have a calendar of my own. And seriously? You change your outgoing message every day? What a waste of time. Wait. I guess you don't change it every day, since it's actually Tuesday, May 14.

"I'll be in meetings most of the day." What does that mean? You won't get back to me? You might get back to me? You're really important because you're in a lot of meetings? I shouldn't have called and bothered you? And what about "most" of the day—how many hours is that?

"I'm unavailable to take your call right now" (or the dreaded "I'm away from my desk right now"). I guess that makes sense, being that I got your voice mail. You mean you're not sitting right there waiting for my call? Guess I'm not that important. And I hate leaving a voice mail for you. I never know when or even *if* you'll call me back.

"Please leave a message, and I'll call you as soon as possible." Okay. "Hi, it's me; call me back." I'm sure I'll hear back from you within an hour because that's what ASAP means to me. But to you? Two days. Sigh. Oh, and I didn't tell you what I need, which *guarantees* you won't ever call me back.

We're all busy gleefully reading research studies on
face-to-face communication and reading body language
(after all, it's our weapon for ensuring everyone is physically in the office where we can monitor them!). We're
combing through articles on the importance of high-
fiving each other at the stand-up meeting every morning
at 8:30 AM sharp. We're judging people for their work
styles and frantically writing policies on how, when, and
where people should communicate most effectively. And
through all of this, we've overlooked the most obvious
communication showstoppers.

Like the outgoing voice mail mentioned previously.
Let's rework it. Let's make it communicate effectively:

"Hi, this is Bill. Please leave me a detailed message
about what you need and when you need it by, and I
will respond. You can also reach out to [backup
person @ backup person's phone number]."

In this scenario, you haven't droned on about the date
and your endless meetings. You haven't given the subtle
but deadly and *untrue* message that you're unavailable.
Instead, your outgoing communication gets both you and
the customer/coworker what *you* need so that you can
get the caller what *he or she* needs. As the customer, I know
that when I call you and I get *your* voice mail, I need to be
clear about what *I* need and when I need it by so that you
can effectively serve my needs.

If you're Bill, you're not getting any more vague or
cryptic messages that paralyze you into doing nothing.

And this solves the back and forth, cutesy "Tag, you're it" voice mail game: "Hey, you called! Just returning your call . . . you're it!"

Don't worry too much about whether the back-up person you offered up will be able to respond fast enough if the customer or coworker uses that option. The point is, you're giving the customer/coworker another *choice*. Most of the time, customers/coworkers will leave a message because the need isn't life-threatening or urgent—and they can wait.

Of course, there are going to be situations where you won't be accessing your voice mail as usual. You may be on vacation, or for whatever reason not responding like you *normally* would. This is when you must alert your callers that your *response time* will be changing:

> *Old outgoing message:* "Hi, this is Bill. I will be on vacation September 3–7. If you need assistance while I'm gone, contact [backup name @ backup phone number]."

> *Customer-focused outgoing message that communicates effectively:* "Hi, this is Bill. I will be responding to voice mails beginning Monday, September 10. Please leave me a detailed message with what you need and when you need it by, and I will respond. If you need assistance prior to the 10th, contact [backup name @ backup phone number]."

At first glance, these may appear to be equally effective. However, the value of the second one lies in the subtleties. It doesn't matter to customers/coworkers where you are; they just want to know when you're going to respond. This also allows you to avoid judgment: "You're on vacation again? How many vacation days do you get, anyway?" Also, the old message doesn't help you or clients/coworkers get what you or they need. It's off-putting, and they're likely to think: "I don't feel like I can leave a message. Better wait until you return. But then you'll be bombarded. Geez. I'll never get what I need. And I don't want to go to the backup. Do I have to?"

With the old message, Bob effectively protected himself by shutting out customers and coworkers. With the new message, Bob projected the attitude, "I will respond—just tell me what you need. My alter ego is working for me even when I'm unplugged."

It's clear—and even more important, it's focused on the customer.

The same works for your bounce-back e-mail reply, fondly referred to as your "out of office" response. This is another one of your alter egos, working tirelessly for you and the customer 24/7. And it's a great tool to let people know when your response time is changing and you won't be responding as usual.

People use their "out of office" in the most unusual and puzzling ways. We get it; it's important to *be* important. Here are a couple of my favorites:

Crazy out of office reply #1: I will be visiting our Washington office March 21–25, and will be in meetings for most of the week. If this is urgent, you can reach me on my mobile, although I will have limited access to phone and e-mail both while traveling and during meetings. Thank you for your patience as I get back to you!

Customer Interpretation: Okay. So you'll be in meetings most of the week just like you are when you're in the "home office." Not feeling so good about that if I have an urgent need or request. You'll have limited access to phone and e-mail. Does that mean you'll be in the mountains with no service? Are you leaving your phone somewhere, or will you have it with you? How patient do I need to be with my *urgent* request? Do you even *care?*

■ ■ ■

Crazy Out of Office Reply #2: Hi there! I'm traveling a bunch this week, so I may be slow responding to e-mail and phone messages. Thanks for your patience. Cheers!

Customer Interpretation: Okay. So you're traveling this week. In other words, you have a great excuse for a slow response. By the way, how "slow" might you be? Should I just assume you'll be unable to respond (those pesky airports—they just aren't conducive to responding to e-mails). Wait. Isn't this the twenty-first century? And I *always* have to be patient with you. If it's not travel, it's some other lame excuse. Like you're booked in a lot of meetings. I really don't care if you're traveling. I still have a need. Are you going to take care of it? And "cheers"?! Yeah, I sure could use a beer about now.

Cali: This is exactly how I felt about someone I had to deal with a couple of years ago—and I remember the situation vividly. (Unfortunately, Jody wouldn't let me have a beer *every* time I got upset about the situation; I guess I should thank her because I might still be suffering from the effects of that.) Every time I needed something from this particular person, she would e-mail me back and say, "I'll be traveling for the next week/I'm traveling right now/I'm leaving tomorrow on business, so it might take awhile to get back on this." I would think "So you're traveling back to 1870, where you can't communicate when you step away from your electric telegraph?!?

Let's be clear: if you're traveling, in meetings, or at a conference, you're *working*. Think of the boy who cried wolf. If you use your out of office e-mail reply for every little thing, people will just think you're lame and will stop reading it. It's not customer-focused; it's *me*-focused. "Look at how busy I am! My company lets me travel! They invite me to a lot of meetings! I'm *so important!*"

Use your out of office e-mail response only in the instances you'll *truly* be nonresponsive for an extended period of time—like during vacation. Customers will actually read it, because they haven't gotten multiple iterations of your bounce-back e-mail on a continual basis. And be clear about when you'll be responding. Nobody cares about the other shit. Trust me.

Crazy Out of Office Reply #3: Hi, I love working for XYZ Company. This place is absolutely amazing and has a mission that is driven by an incredible group of committed people called XYZ Company Coordinators. They inspire me by working so hard to make such a difference in the lives of others that I do all that I can to support their efforts. Even so, I've decided that it's time to take a little vacation and will be out of the office through Friday, April 13. I will try to respond to your e-mail while away but have a packed schedule and may not have a chance to do this. Still, if you really need to get in touch with me just call or text me at [phone] whenever it is convenient for you. I'll do my best to get back to you as quickly as possible. For anything related to Human Resources or Operations, please also try to contact [name] at [e-mail]. For anything related to training, please contact [name], [e-mail].

Customer Interpretation: SERIOUSLY? Who's going to read this overblown, overdone message and not think, "What a suck-up"? "I love my job so much! But alas, I *must* go on vacation. However, I'm so dedicated, I'll try to respond to you even though my vacation is jam-packed with activities!" *Gag.* Whatever.

The following is a good example of a *customer-focused* out of office response:

I will be responding to e-mails beginning Monday, April 15. Please respond to this e-mail and let me know what you need and when you need it by. If you need assistance before April 15, please contact [back-up person's e-mail/phone].

It's clear. And it's not filled with socially acceptable "get out of work free" excuses.

Now that you know your alter egos have your back 24/7 and that your job is to *respond*, you can let go of the stressful notion that you are available and can never unplug. You can. You just have to manage unplugging in a customer-focused manner through communicating changes in your response time.

Now if the boss calls at 8:00 PM and you're having dinner with your family, you can continue bringing that forkful of pot roast to your lips. Voice mail has you covered. And it's okay to call or e-mail someone at 3:00 in the morning or noon on a Saturday, even though the person may be at the grocery store or taking a nap. You can still keep the flow of communication going by leaving a voice mail or e-mail. Waiting until 8 AM on Monday morning is old thinking.

Communicating outside of traditional office hours using alter egos is how work moves along today—and it doesn't mean anything. It doesn't mean you're a harder worker or more dedicated to the company if you e-mail at 3:00 in the morning. You're not going to get an award for setting all of your e-mails to go out at 1 AM, 3 AM, and 6 AM. You're not more promotable if you leave a voice mail for a coworker on Saturday. We all know that trick.

If only it were that simple.

Now, you still have to manage communication when you find yourself in the physical workplace. We may believe that the best communication happens in the office or that the best relationships are formed here. But then why do we still feel frustrated? Why can't we get anything done? Why do we have to *leave* the workplace to *work*?

You've heard it a million times, and we've all been there. You perceive that you can get 8 hours of work done in 4 hours when you work from home. Or the coffee shop. Or the cabin. You relish in your productivity. You high-five yourself from your deck . . . or dock. Why? Because you're in a place where you can manage those pesky interruptions we believe are the best forms of communication. Spontaneous. Necessary. Make businesses sing!

There you are, in the office, and for the umpteenth time trying to get yourself on task when yet another coworker comes sauntering by your workstation to ask you a question. They have just one *little* question . . . "Do you have a minute?" You grit your teeth and force out a smile. What are you supposed to say? You've already been interrupted. And if you scream out, "Leave me alone! Can't you see I'm trying to work here?" you'll get reprimanded for not living the company values. You know the ones. Respect. Humility. Integrity. Family.

We like to refer to this artifact from the days of yore as a drive-by. It is the physical act of getting up, walking over to someone's workstation, and starting a conversation. You might need to get a quick answer so that *you* can keep your work flowing. You may be bored and need a break. You *prefer* face-to-face communication. You believe the recipient of the drive-by won't understand your e-mail; you have to wave your arms around to get your point across. You may have to ramp up your facial expressions, voice inflections. "At first, we struggled with changing how we communicate in the office," says Susan Hoaby, "We were afraid of being blamed for doing a drive-by!"

But from the perspective of the person being "driven upon," it's a whole different story. That person feels interrupted and annoyed—and probably wasn't equipped to answer your question on the spot. That person isn't bored and doesn't care to talk about your wild weekend at the moment. The timing is off. It's all about *you*.

The physical office is a flurry of drive-bys, because, let's face it, who can sit around for 8 hours without moving around? And, if you're stuck there anyway and don't feel like working at the moment, surely someone nearby will accommodate you, right?

"The increased organization and setting of dead-lines/timelines has brought clarity and a sense of inten-tion to the team," says Learner's Edge executive director Julie Yaeger. "This was a challenge for all of us, as we functioned using more of a quick drive-by, random check-in sort of method, which worked due to our size but wasn't as respectful of others' time and responsibili-ties. We now place our deadlines on a shared calendar in Outlook, which allows me to have a strong grasp of what is on each team member's plate as well as each task's priority."

Driving by someone's workstation is the *old* way of doing things. It's couched as efficient, when it's actually

undermining productivity. For every person who's interrupted, it's like throwing sand on the bike gears of business. People are being brought to a screeching halt a
million times a day in offices all over the world. The
physical drive-by puts all the power into the driver's hands.
The person being driven upon is at the driver's whim,
without the ability to manage the flow of communication
or prepare for the encounter. In effect? They're trapped.

Can an e-mail or a phone call be a drive-by?

Let's say you're sitting in the office doing work.
Instead of someone physically coming over to your
workstation and interrupting you, that person sends you
an e-mail telling you what's needed. Now you're in
control. You can respond to that e-mail on your terms.
And because you can read the e-mail when you're not put
on the spot, you can *respond* in a thoughtful, calm manner.

The person who sent the e-mail gets what he or she
needs. You manage the communication. And the same
goes for voice-mail. You are in control.

So the next time you want to wallow in the days
where managers subscribed to "management by wandering around," *stop*. Think about what you need. Send
off an e-mail or leave a voice mail instead of doing a
drive-by and interrupting the flow of work. Be specific
and clear in your e-mail or voice mail about what you
need, and trust that you'll get a response. And if you can't
live without seeing the person face to face for your
question or need, still send an e-mail or leave a voice mail.
Let that person know you'd like to meet face to face. Ask
when it would be convenient for that person to meet.

Oh, and don't put on your running shoes.

One of our favorite stories from the field is from an employee who gave us his interpretation of *sneakernet* as a way to communicate. Wikipedia defines it as "a tongue-in-cheek sound-alike to ethernet, and refers to someone wearing sneakers as the transport mechanism for the data." This employee described it as a method someone uses to get your attention if you don't respond to an e-mail within 5 minutes. That person puts on some sneakers and runs over to your workstation.

Cali: If you think sneakernet is crazy, get this one: Back when we were at Best Buy, certain teams would put signs across the openings to their cubes that said, "Working for the customer—don't interrupt." This was obviously an attempt to say, "Leave me alone, or I'll snap into a million pieces." The response to the sign from those driving by? Some would hum a little tune as they proceeded to limbo under the sign, some would move it to one side and walk right in, and some would give it a big ol' karate chop and say, "I can see you have this up, but I just have one quick question. . . ."

E-mail and voice mail have been around long enough for us to use as tools—our alter egos—and using the tips in this chapter, we can manage them effectively to get our needs and the needs of our clients or coworkers met. But what about instant messaging? Skype? Texting? Social media? Wait a minute! What about that control we thought we had?

You can make a decision about what communication tool, from synchronous to asynchronous, will work best to accomplish what you need to accomplish for any kind of business need. Synchronous tools enable real-time communication and collaboration in a same time–different place mode. They allow people to connect at a single point in time, at the same time, and include things like instant messaging, phone conferencing, and Skyping. Asynchronous tools enable communication and collaboration over a period of time through a different time–different place mode. These tools allow people to connect together at each person's own convenience and own schedule; they include e-mail, voice mail, and texting.

Before you begin a communication, consider which tool is the most effective for getting what you need in terms of the work. E-mail works great for communicating objective information; however, it sucks for complex, emotional discussions. I'll never forget the day I received my two-week notice by e-mail. That sucked *big* time.

Instant messaging is a great tool for getting quick answers or having short conversations. It can become an annoying electronic drive-by situation if people don't honor your Busy or Do Not Disturb status. We were working at a company that had an open workspace design that was a drive-by breeding ground. They decided to use their instant messaging status to indicate when it was okay to interrupt them with a physical drive-by. Red?

Stay away. Green? Come on over! This worked because everyone agreed to do it. They *communicated* and didn't just assume it wouldn't work. And, they held each other accountable to it. They didn't need a policy.

Texting works great if you have to shoot off a quick "I'm almost there" update. Cali and I use texting when we're communicating something that needs to rise above the fray of everything else. If she sends me an e-mail that I need to attend to first above all, she'll text me "See e-mail about XYZ." Or, if there's an urgent need, I get a text. For us, and for many other people, texting trumps all other communication in the moment.

Of course, we all are painfully aware that communication can break down. This can even happen if we're all sitting face to face. People misinterpret body language all the time. Face to face is not a guarantee that communication will be effective. Sometimes technology fails us. You may find yourself in a videoconferencing situation in which the application simply doesn't work or your Internet connection fails. In these situations, you may have to default to a conference call.

With a buffet of communication options, the most important thing to remember is that you are communicating because you need something in order to achieve your results. Getting frustrated with technology and forcing everyone into the office because that is *your* preferred way of communicating is not the answer. And neither is managing people's communication *for* them.

The following example is well worth mentioning as one of the biggest blunders of all time. It is exactly the kind of seriously misguided nonsense we are going to have to overcome in the next decade. And this company can kiss good-bye any chance that they will be able to recruit or retain the next generation of workers.

In an article posted in December 2011, Volkswagen (VW) decided that BlackBerries were going to "punch out" 30 minutes after workers had punched out and then "punch back in" 30 minutes before employees punched back in. The company had worked out a deal with unionized workers at its German sites to eliminate their postwork BlackBerry use. Someone at VW had the brilliant idea that turning off people's ability to communicate would alleviate the tendency for employees to feel that they are chained to their smartphones and to let those pesky bosses know that it's naughty to communicate after hours. They go on to say that maybe some workers who want to access information might be allowed access after hours. You see where this is going, right?

Here's the bright side. VW employees at the German sites will still be able to use their BlackBerries during that critical 2 to 3 PM hour when mobile phone use typically spikes during dull afternoon meetings. Yeah! Thanks, VW!

You couldn't pay me a salary high enough to work at a company that is so seriously out of touch. Remember our alter egos e-mail and voice mail? Could it be that workers at VW didn't feel like they had control over their response time? That the reason they felt chained was cultural, not technical? It seems that VW decided to use a technical solution to a cultural problem. They opted to make decisions about how adults use their own communication devices. The solution, however, isn't to cut people off at the knees. VW might have been better off digging deeper into the culture. They may have discovered tired old management practices that caused managers to exhibit paternalistic behaviors over adults, like managing their employees' communication "after hours" because obviously they couldn't manage it themselves.

I wonder if *management's* BlackBerries had to punch out after hours.

Communication and teamwork aren't things that you achieve by having everyone sit in the same place at the same time. Being a team isn't stimulated *best* by proximity. A team forms to respond to a common goal, outcome, or business need. We're fortunate to live in a time where we have a variety of tools that can facilitate synchronous and asynchronous communication and collaboration.

We need to stop managing how people communicate and collaborate and make sure everyone understands the measurable results that need to be achieved. Communicate *that* effectively, and you're golden.

Okay. Gotta go. I'm going to physically unplug now, but you can expect me to respond to business needs as usual. My alter egos never unplug. Nice.

Typical Questions

The following are typical questions managers ask when they're thinking about a ROWE for their team or organization. These questions are important because evolving to a ROWE requires a different way of solving common challenges. Lose no sleep! Here are the answers.

Q: What if I like face-to-face communication best? Don't my employees need to respect that?

A: It depends. If you're going to slow down productivity, then *you're* being disrespectful, not them. Make sure you choose face-to-face interaction for situations where it makes the most sense to achieve measurable results. Be open to communicating using other means. If you give your employees the freedom to choose from a plethora of communication tools, they will choose face-to-face *if* the situation calls for it. If you force them to communicate in your style *only*, you've lost them. And your engagement scores will show it.

Q: We have lots of last-minute fire drills. I need people to be available during standard office hours.

A: The first response I have to this is, Why do you have a lot of last-minute fire drills? Is it because of poor planning? We know some fire drills in business are unavoidable, but a business that runs on putting out fires has a deeper issue. In terms of availability, use the phone and embrace voice mail and e-mail. People will respond.

Q: What do I do if someone doesn't respond?

A: If someone doesn't respond, communicate your need to their backup. In some cases, you'll have to make a decision or take action without the other person's response. If the other person is nonresponsive for days and hasn't indicated a change in response time using his or her outgoing voice mail message or out of office e-mail reply, you have a performance issue to deal with.

Q: I think it's important and courteous for people to communicate where they're working from if they're not going to be in the office.

A: Why? Do you need to know where the e-mail servers and voice mail servers are located, too? Are you afraid people might be—gasp—*not* working if they're not in the workplace? Think about what you need and reach out. Pick up the phone, leave a voice mail, or shoot off an e-mail. It doesn't matter where people are working *from*. What matters is that the work is getting done. If people need to communicate where they're working from during traditional office hours, you're just reinforcing that this is when (and where) work *should* happen. And you're definitely not a ROWE. You don't make people tell you where they're working from on nights and weekends, do you? Silly.

Things to Try

1. Go 1 full week without doing a single drive-by. Get what you need another way.
2. Use a form of communication that you've been avoiding, such as instant messaging or Skyping.
3. Work from another location without using your out-of-office e-mail response.
4. Change your outgoing voice mail message and get the other members of your team to do the same thing.

(continued)

(continued)

5. Pick a couple of the face-to-face meetings on your calendar and choose to communicate a different way to get to the same result.

Things to Avoid

1. Driving in rush hour traffic. You don't have to be in the physical office at 8 AM and leave at 5 PM to communicate effectively.

2. Changing your outgoing voice mail message incessantly to let everyone know irrelevant stuff like the calendar date.

3. Using communication tools that don't fit the situation—for example, e-mailing a time-sensitive, urgent request. Text or leave a voice mail instead. Not all people get e-mail on their mobile phones.

4. Instant messaging coworkers who have set their status to "Busy" with a nonurgent message. They're *busy*. E-mail instead.

5. Managing people's communication *style*. Just because you want to see everyone's shiny, happy faces gathered around you, it's not always effective, practical, or efficient.

Get Support!

Visit www.gorowe.com/training to learn more about the Beyond Telework for Managers Workshop or to schedule a culture assessment.

Focus on What Matters

by Greg Watt

Greg Watt is the president and chief executive officer of WATT Publishing, located in Rockford, Illinois. Established in 1917, WATT is a media company that provides business-to-business knowledge and information to the agribusiness industry. According to Watt, "We bring buyers and sellers in the poultry, pig, feed, and pet food industries together with our leading content distributed through a wide array of media channels."

WATT Publishing began its journey to a Results-Only Work Environment (ROWE) in March 2012 with CultureRx's on-site Leadership Summit. The company went on to establish a ROWE through CultureRx's on-site training in May 2012.

Since we implemented a ROWE, we have, for the first time, total staff alignment on the clear definition of our customer, what our ultimate business outcome is, and how each employee's goals and objectives fit with our business's strategic outcomes. This was a company-wide collaboration on these conclusions through our ROWE, another first for us. Although it sounds crazy, defining the customer is no small accomplishment in our business. Many companies in business-to-business media, including ours, have endured a long-time disagreement between different departments on who the ultimate customer is. Ask senior management from three media companies, and you're likely to get three different answers. This lack of clarity can lead to inefficiencies

(continued)

(continued)

and conflict throughout the system, which clearly results in a less-than-ideal outcome for the customer.

We also used CultureRx's Outcome-Based Goal-Setting Platform and received conclusive feedback from our company-wide collaboration on the following:

- What *activities enable* the outcome?
- What *activities do not enable* the outcome?
- How will we *measure success*?

This company-wide collaborative process also allowed us to have everyone now focused on how we measure success: by ensuring financial stability and company growth. Activities that achieve success include, among other things, meeting and exceeding individual and department goals, meeting and exceeding strategic initiatives, and increasing reader engagement and growing audience. We are also in the process of implementing new organizational measurements to monitor our success.

This new mind-set of focusing on the results led us to review all individual employees' goals and objectives with each of the managers. Each set of individual goals are tied back to the department goals and are required to be connected with one or more of the corporate strategic goals. We discovered during the review process that although some goals and objectives were written with excellent clarity and focused time-lines and that others were good with some room for improvement, a few needed a lot of work. We provided feedback and coaching with each of the managers to bring each staff person's goals closer to having crystal-clear outcomes. This will be a tremendous benefit to all of our staff and ultimately to our customer.

As part of our on-site training with CultureRx, we were tasked with a specific set of instructions to "Do something scary." This activity required us to behave in a way we would not normally behave. For example, an employee who has come into the workplace at 8 AM sharp for 30 years, was now tasked with coming in at 10 AM one day without telling anyone. Another employee was tasked with working from another location other than the workplace without informing their manager. We were seriously pushing up against old beliefs and ingrained beha-viors. The feedback that we got through our cor-porate intranets' staff postings has been a lot of fun for everyone—and fulfilling to me personally that our staff is really valuing being in a ROWE! Many employees' quality of work/life balance has been measurably impacted in a very positive way. Several staff have shared their *Why Work Sucks and How to Fix It* book with family and friends, and the con-versation always leads to the same reaction: "I wish *my* company would do this!"

(*continued*)

(*continued*)

Of course, a ROWE requires significant change, and it really challenged some managers to fully trust their staff to attain the results they need, even if they are not present at their desk. Our new mind-set is: "Work is what we do, not where we go," and we recognize that this may be in a nontraditional location during a nontraditional time. The management team no longer gives kudos to anyone who sends the report or an e-mail at 2 AM. It's about the result the action achieves, not when the action is taken. It's also a culture shift from reactive to proactive.

For some, this meant a significant shift to being a coach from their previous role as a command and control manager. This will take additional training to fully implement and be effective.

Although we considered ourselves to be ROWE "lite" in how we operated previously, we discovered unknown "Sludge" (snarky comments about how people were spending their time like 'Has anyone seen Jim? He's always late!') in the company, which came forward in the workshop. The workshop provided information that was both eye-opening and enlightening. Being in an *official* ROWE led our home office staff to feel immediate relief. They knew they no longer needed to be tied down to their desk and available at any time for that random call. Additionally, our office staff no longer operates according to the mind-set that "home office" employees have it better. Everyone is now the same; *they* make the choice about where and when to work.

We've now empowered *all* staff to question processes and procedures that don't provide value to the outcome. This improved feedback has been especially beneficial on all levels of communication. In other words, we question any communication that lacks clarity to make sure it's written or spoken with everyone understanding and in agreement. We've vastly improved meeting agendas with focus and results objectives, and we put more careful thought into who is invited to make sure all present *need* to be there.

Establishing individual goals is now a two-way dialogue between the employee and his or her manager, who reviews and resets these goals every 120 days. We had just begun implementing this prior to committing to a ROWE, and our new structure has helped crystalize the process for everyone.

Although seemingly simple, it's been helpful and much more productive for all to understand that there are many ways to communicate with one another depending on the need. Whether through Skype, e-mail, text, or mobile or land line, there are various options—certain ones that are better than others when the caller/sender thinks first about the message's need and priority. The net result has been

(continued)

(continued)

fewer unnecessary interruptions, and our customers and staff are receiving the benefits.

When asked, "Why should a company get training to adopt a ROWE?" I think the better question is, "Why would any company *not* go through training to adopt an authentic ROWE?" Why would they continue to perform any activity or activities that do not meet individual and department goals aligned with the strategic plan? Why not empower everyone to question unnecessary or inefficient activities, including poor communication, fire drills, lack of adherence to deadlines, unproductive meetings, and lack of clear goals/outcomes or scope on project ideas? Being in a ROWE is so basic, yet some managers and senior leaders simply refuse to let go of their alleged power silos.

WATT is a 90+-year-old, fourth-generation, family-owned, and family-led business. We have a good mix of employees with tenure from less than a year to more than 30 years. Some were skeptical of the ROWE concept when we announced it at the company-wide workshop. However, the due diligence we did in researching ROWE—first with senior leadership, followed by a full management training by CultureRx prior to committing fully company-wide—gave us the confidence that ROWE *would* succeed at WATT. We made it clear to everyone in the company that everyone in leadership was fully committed to this. Once we completed the company-wide ROWE workshop with CultureRx—and now after 90 days into our adoption—*everyone* is embracing the ROWE.

Admittedly, it's hard to change a company culture. But with a ROWE and training from the experts at CultureRx, we've noticeably shifted WATT's culture into a company-wide team that is all looking at the same result. We're developing a workforce that is a real strategic advantage in the marketplace.

CHAPTER

5

No More Bullshit Meetings. Period.

Meetings. They look like work. They feel like work. They smell like work. There's nothing like getting the team around a conference table, batting around random thoughts to make sure everyone is on the same page. And you never know when a good topic or idea will mightily rise up out of conference table dust! Plus, there isn't a single technology substitute that lends itself to reading body language in terms of effective communication like being physically face to face. You can't do that in an e-mail or on a conference call. And that Skype thing is just too impersonal. Also, I can never get it to work.

Huh?

People all over the globe tell us they waste anywhere from 30 to 80 percent of their time in unproductive meetings. Although someone feels (for whatever reason) that these meetings are vitally important to the work, most participants feel like it's such a waste of time that it requires blood pressure medication just to get through it. There are so many bad meetings that even if a meeting is good, we're so burned out from the ineffective ones that we can hardly muster up the energy to be excited.

Meetings dominate the way we do business today. According to a network MCI Conferencing white paper titled "Meetings in America: A study of trends, costs and attitudes toward business travel, teleconferencing, and their impact on productivity," approximately 11 million meetings occur in the United States each and every day. Most professionals attend a total of 61.8 meetings per month. The research also indicates that more than 50 percent of this meeting time is wasted. Even *more* frightening is the fact that, according to the study, most professionals who meet on a regular basis admit to day-dreaming (91 percent), missing meetings (96 percent), or missing parts of meetings (95 percent). A large percentage (73 percent) say they have brought other work to meetings, and 39 percent say they have dozed during meetings.

A separate study by career site Salary.com on workplace time drains found that "Too many meetings" was the number 1 time waster at the office, cited by 47 percent of 3,164 workers, up from 42 percent in 2008.

Let's put it bluntly: *meetings suck.*

Throughout the past century, before and after the advent of communication technology advances, face-to-face meetings have been the default way to communicate, collaborate, and get everyone aligned. And we continue to believe that they're a necessary evil to make sure collaboration is effective. We believe work gets done in meetings and that more work comes out of them. We even believe the best relationships are built face to face and that these are the ones that drive business. Even Dictionary.com implies in their definition of a meeting that they must somehow be a *physical* gathering:

1. the act of coming together: *a chance meeting in the park.*
2. an assembly or conference of personas for a specific purpose: *a ten o'clock business meeting.*
3. the body of persons present at an assembly or conference: *to read a report to the meeting.*

It's natural to think in terms of people sitting together in the same place when reading these definitions.

And then there's the infamous impromptu meeting: you get up, walk over to someone else's workstation, and immediately begin addressing a topic for which you've given the person no notice whatsoever. Remember the drive-by communication tactic mentioned in Chapter 4? After all, if you need a quick answer, you can just get up and go get it, right? If you need to eliminate ambiguity by using dramatic voice inflection or communicate the urgency of your need, drive by! And when you feel the need for a little human interaction in your communication, drive by. Then, you don't actually have to put a real meeting on the calendar. Much more efficient—for *you.*

Of course, you've now managed to interrupt, annoy, and throw off track the person being "driven-upon." And worst of all, that person's not able to prepare for what you need. Caught off guard, this person is pulled into your impromptu meeting without having any say in it at all. And even if the person says, "Please don't interrupt me right now," it's too late, because you've already interrupted.

Cali: I love the organizations that say, "We have this under control. We're able to tell each other if we just don't have time to discuss something when they stop by." But like Jody said, the interruption has already happened—and *this* is what so many people don't understand! The damage is already done the second you tear my attention away from what I'm already focused on. You're no better than the organization next door that has 15-minute conversations every time a drive-by happens. An interruption is an interruption.

And let's not forget the prairie dog meeting, the one where you stand up and yell across other people's workstations to get your question answered and pull other unsuspecting, unprepared, uninterested people into your meeting. But at least your needs were met, right?

The ineffectiveness of meetings has become so prevalent that a whole army of consultants and critical thinkers has come up with a zillion ways to make meetings more effective. They've come up with tools and tactics such as effectiveness checklists, protocols, rules of engagement, ways to write effective agendas, decrees on whom to invite and whom not to invite, meeting room logistics (including best lighting and temperature to get everyone psyched and keep them alert), time management guidelines, and how to be respectful, polite, and add value. And you could hear a battle cry all over the planet with the introduction of conference calling. Now we can develop a whole slew of new protocols for conference call meetings! Especially because the people who get to conference in somehow become less important than the people who are really present at the meeting . . . the ones around the conference table. Jim? Did you just say something? Oh yeah. We have people on the phone. Better put their names up on the whiteboard so we include them. And we'd better have human resources write some more guidelines.

It's exhausting. And people continue to complain about wasting time, resources, and their lives in boring, ineffective, senseless, politically charged, chest-puffing meetings. There's really no work getting done at all, or as efficiently as we know it can, and we feel overworked, overwhelmed, and cheated. Not only did I sit in meeting after meeting all day, now I have to go home and do my *real* work while my spouse, partner, friends, or kids look at me with pity—or worse, anger and contempt.

Eric Severson, senior vice president, Gap North America, used CultureRx's proven process to implement a Results-Only Work Environment (ROWE) in the Outlet Division in 2008. Severson was working on a number of things to improve the work/life equation for his people, but he did so much more by adopting a ROWE. He says:

> I was hoping to alleviate the long, senseless commutes my younger staff [members] were experiencing [having to drive] to and from the Bay Area [every day]. I didn't anticipate the profound effect it would have on making meetings actually work. The more focused [and] respectful of the work and people's time and lives we became, the better we got at knowing when a meeting was really necessary. The senseless recurring meetings dropped off our calendars first, followed by a number of status update and staff meetings that we realized were not helping us achieve our measurable results. A meeting is just a tool. And now we know how to use it effectively.

Advances in technology have allowed today's meetings to take many forms. And instant messaging or Skype conversations between two or more people can be *characterized* as a meeting.

But no matter what form your meeting takes, every meeting should have one thing in common: it should be your *last* option for achieving what you need to achieve. In other words, you have a meeting only if you've concluded that there is no other way to accomplish the work or get what you need—and most important, *every single person or persons involved wholeheartedly agrees with you.*

"We effectively eliminated 2,000 'man hours' of meetings within the first 3 months of our ROWE training conducted by CultureRx," says Susan Hoaby, president of Minneapolis-based retail consulting company JL Buchanan. "The significance for us as a small business was that the elimination of nonproductive meeting time equated to the salary of one full-time employee!"

I once worked at a large corporation where our team had a full-day, recurring mandatory meeting every month. Everyone on the team was expected to attend. It was meant to get everyone motivated and on the same page and was a meeting that a consultant suggested would help us collaborate, build closer relationships, and share pertinent updated information. It was a way for leadership to be visible to inspire, guide, and motivate us. And *not* attending the meeting created so much guilt, you'd never even *think* of skipping out.

Recurring meetings can be—and often are—*huge* time wasters. They create a block of time that you and your colleagues must then *fill in some way*.

The two days preceding the big mandatory meeting, everyone was either (1) running around like crazy trying to prepare what they had to present, pinging off all other team members like a pinball machine on steroids interrupting the real work, or (2) dreading the upcoming mandatory meeting and beginning to fake "coming down with a cold" so that if they didn't attend, they could pull the "I was ill" card.

Wait. How can it be *mandatory* if you can use certain excuses to get out of it?

I took a notice of who didn't attend one of these meetings. I knew that these people were in the office, but for some reason weren't present in that room. What gives, I wondered? I thought it was *mandatory*. So I boldly asked a couple of these suspiciously absent people why they didn't attend (my bad, since they were my superiors). They answered by informing me that they had to attend to customer needs. Really? So did a lot of the rest of us in the mandatory meeting who didn't have the hierarchical weight to use that excuse.

So now we had two acceptable excuses:

1. I'm sick (called in sick *or* at workstation sick and don't want to pass germs to everyone in the meeting . . . cough, cough).
2. I'm taking care of business (that is, important enough to get a free pass).

The 2 days after the mandatory meeting, there was a flurry of complaining, lamenting, and teeth gnashing about how much time we wasted in it and the lack of value it added to our work. We contemplated how we could get out of the next one. But whether we were spending time in the meeting or just complaining about it, the one thing we *weren't* doing was working.

So there were basically 5 days when we experienced a serious loss of productivity: 2 days before while we scrambled to get ready, 1 day to meet, and 2 days to complain.

Let's do the math. There were approximately 200 people expected to attend the mandatory full-day meeting monthly, with an average salary of $50,000. If all 200 attended, the salary cost for 1 day was $38,461. Now do that each month for 12 months and the salary cost is a whopping $461,532.

And this math didn't account for the productivity loss both during the meeting and for the 4 days surrounding it. It didn't represent the cost for the room, continental breakfast, mid-morning snacks, boxed lunches, mid-afternoon snacks and continually flowing beverages.

Now that's just one meeting per month with 200 people. Think of all the meetings going on day after day, hour after hour, with resources who agree that 30 to 80 percent is wasted time—er, money. And no amount of meeting effectiveness trainings or lists of meeting protocols has fixed it—in *decades*.

Some organizations who have tried to fix the overwhelming amount of meetings by designating a period of time where no meetings should take place, say "No-meeting Thursdays." The challenge is that the culture still *believes* that meetings are necessary to get work done, collaborate, communicate, and so on. So these organizations simply hold more meetings on the remaining 4 days, or people have forbidden "secret meetings" on no-meeting days. A no-meeting day is a technical fix to a deeper problem.

Yet it's possible to remedy this broken relic from the days of yore once and for all. All you have do is this:

Make *every* meeting optional, even the mandatory ones or those where the organizer is the vice president, manager, or some other hierarchically important person. Status update meetings are optional. Stand-up morning meetings are optional. Staff meetings are, too.

Cali: It's normal to have a surprised or even negative reaction to this last paragraph. One of my favorite off-the-cuff responses to "Every meeting is optional" came from a Fortune 100 company vice president who went stark-raving mad, turned bright red, pounded his fist on the table, and yelled, "Every meeting will *not* be optional!" That same week, a senior vice president at the same company left a meeting (and slammed the door loud enough to make a picture fall off the wall) where we were discussing how "Every meeting is optional" comes to life. His parting comment: "People can't make these decisions about meetings—we're not a *democracy* here!"

The following is bad meeting protocol that's become accepted, albeit irritating, in workplaces today:

1. Accepting multiple meetings, then choosing one to go to and not declining the other—or letting the other meeting organizer know you won't be attending.
2. Choosing one meeting over another meeting and not contributing to the meeting you've declined. (What was your role? Why were you invited in the first place? What are you not providing that was needed?)
3. Accepting as "tentative" and never either fully accepting or declining. You're just sitting on the fence, making people wonder what you'll do.

4. Coming to a meeting totally unprepared with a bunch of excuses as to why. You're too overworked or overwhelmed; you have too much on your plate. At least you showed up, right?

5. Multitasking at the meeting. Answering e-mails, texting, and otherwise attending halfway. It's obvious you have better things to do. Go do them.

6. Sitting idly by in a meeting that's going nowhere without speaking up.

Cali: Number 4 is my favorite . . . meaning, of course, that it makes me want to scream. People rushing into meetings who are so late that they'll never know what's going on, and saying, "So sorry! I'm quadruple-booked all day today. Well, actually all week! Mind if I eat? I haven't eaten lunch for the past 3 days. While I chow this down, can I get just a quick recap? What did I miss?" I don't care who you are or who you *think* you are—this is disrespectful of everyone's time and you need to get your "I'm the king/queen" fix somewhere else.

We've all seen it and been frustrated by it. Making every meeting optional does not mean there are *no* meetings or that people will decline every meeting because they hate them. Making every meeting optional does not create a culture of entitled employees who relish in the fact that they can use their power to stick it to the manager.

It's only when you make every single meeting *optional* that a meeting has the fighting chance of being relevant, not to mention effective. And it's been proved effective, not just in theory, but in practice as well. Actual companies are doing this, and it's working.

"Being an engineering and manufacturing company, our ROWE training with CultureRx has exposed several weak spots in our project management and decision-making processes," says Dennis Malecek, president of Dynatronix, an industry leader in the design and manufacture of Pulse, Pulse Reverse, and DC power supplies for the worldwide metal finishing industry. "The best thing we've noticed, in our short time of being a ROWE, is the requirement for everyone to be very clear in their communications. Meetings now have clear agendas. We've changed, even cancelled, some weekly meetings, and have put strict time limits on the ones we do attend."

Most people who receive a meeting invite automatically hit Accept and add it to their calendars. Then we get another and another, and we hit Accept—or maybe just Tentative in case we want to opt out. Besides, responding with Tentative keeps the meeting on our calendar and allows us to see it taking place. Then a meeting invite comes at the same time as another meeting we've already accepted, and we hit Accept again. That way we can make a last-minute decision when it comes time for the meetings. Now we're double and quadruple booked. Two Accepts, two Tentatives. That's because we're so important, and there's so much work and only so many hours in the day!

Bullshit.

The problem is poor planning, believing all the stuff we believe about meetings that isn't true, and accepting meeting mediocrity. It's politics, posturing, and positioning—and it's a big fat waste of time. It gives the person scheduling the meeting ultimate control. Besides, it's not polite to decline a meeting we think is going to be a colossal waste of time, right?

Wrong.

Think about meeting math again. It's our job to *do our jobs*. And part of that is—or should be—using resources effectively and not wasting them.

The task of having a productive meeting falls first in the hands of the person calling it. Before scheduling a meeting, every meeting organizer should answer the following:

1. What do I need exactly?
2. Is what I need relevant to the outcome I or the people I'm working with are trying to achieve?
3. Is having a meeting (whether via instant message, Skype, online meeting, conference call, or in person) the best way to get what I need?
4. Is there a better way to get what I need that uses everyone's time more effectively?
5. Who is an integral part of helping me get what I need?

If you determine that yes, the best way to get what you need is by holding some sort of meeting, then it's up to *you* to convince the people you are inviting that it's a good use of their time, too. They're not just going to blindly accept your meetings anymore.

"As a company, we have focused on more purposeful and clear meetings," says Julie Yaeger of Learner's Edge. "While we were never a company drowning in meetings, we now question the need and make sure the purpose and expectations are clear for all participants."

Slapping together an agenda (just another senseless meeting protocol) will not necessarily convince people whose job it is to not waste time to come to the meeting. Oftentimes, meeting agendas are a list of topics to discuss. Or a list of topics for two people to work through while 15 other people sit idly by and listen. (Ooh! They might hear something interesting! Better invite *everyone* just in case!)

Jessica Lawrence, former chief executive officer (CEO) of the Girl Scouts of San Gorgonio Council, implemented a ROWE in 2008. Before moving to a ROWE, meetings took up a lot of time on everyone's calendars, including hers. And many meetings included 50 percent more people than was really necessary. Lawrence explains, "There's so much that we do every day to [just pass the] time in the workplace, and a meeting is the perfect [place for this]. After we implemented a ROWE and realized that we didn't need to fill time anymore, and we were tasked instead with achieving clear, measurable results, it was like a veil was lifted. We could finally see our way clearly to our purpose without hiding behind a multitude of meetings that, frankly, made us all a little crazy."

Of course, people are going to meet. And if people are not going to waste time and effort, a meeting invite must then have the following elements to clarify why they should spend their time there:

1. The outcome the meeting intends to create (This is critical, because it's what will cause people to agree that a meeting is the best way to accomplish what you're asking—or not.)
2. The role the person you are inviting has in the meeting
3. What each person or the group needs to do to prepare or come prepared to contribute and how it affects the outcome or need for the meeting

If an invitation meets all these conditions, then people will accept it because everyone can readily agree that it's the best way to achieve what's needed.

Declining a meeting if the preceding conditions are not in place is not disrespectful. What's disrespectful is accepting a meeting *knowing* you'll be wasting your time and then wasting even more time talking about the stupid meeting before and after it occurs—or even worse, *accepting it and then not showing up.* Or showing up with lame excuses as to why you're not prepared.

This happened to me once when a senior-level director specifically asked me and some colleagues for a face-to-face meeting. He told me when he wanted the meeting, so I scheduled it and he *accepted* it. I invited the appropriate people to deliver what he needed. We all showed up for the meeting except for . . . you guessed it, the director. The rest of us wasted time preparing for the meeting, showing up for the meeting, and then spending the next 2 hours being unproductive because we were so pissed off.

But back to the previous questions: if you receive a meeting invite that doesn't answer those questions, send a note to the meeting organizer before you decline, asking, "What is the desired outcome of this meeting? What is my role? What can I do to prepare? Is there a better way to achieve the outcome?"

Transformation can occur if everyone commits to always questioning the meeting organizer if these conditions aren't met. Pretty soon, people will know that those elements have to be in place. No results to be expected? No meeting.

When Fairview Foundation, an organization that builds philanthropic partnerships to further Minneapolis-based Fairview Health Services' mission of improving the health of the communities they serve, underwent CultureRx's ROWE training in December 2010, the number of revenue-generating meetings actually *increased*. But the key here is "revenue generating." The focus on what really mattered—*results*—was now on top of everyone's mind.

Every meeting that is optional *does exactly the opposite* of what we might anticipate it will do. It makes everyone accountable for reducing wasted time and for making decisions regarding whether a scheduled meeting is really the best way to drive results. It makes people who attend meetings "show up" fully present because they've come willingly, knowing that the meeting truly is the best way to accomplish what is necessary. They support the outcome and truly understand their role and why their participation is critical.

But this is where, as managers, we have to ask ourselves, (1) Do we *trust* our people to make the right decisions on how to use their time effectively against the results they are tasked to achieve? and (2) Is everyone clear about the outcome and how to measure it (see Chapter 3)?

It's not about trust needing to be *earned*. There will always be a multitude of reasons to not trust someone. But you can't argue with performance against clearly defined, measurable results. If someone is unclear and declines a meeting that is critical to achieving agreed-upon results, it's a performance issue (hence Cali's ranting in Chapter 2). And making the meeting *mandatory* is a sloppy way of taking ownership of something that eliminates your employee's accountability for what they were hired to do. The only thing that's mandatory is producing measurable results (hence the paycheck).

Meetings are one thing: a tool to get to results. If the tool is not doing the job of getting you to results, you're using the wrong tool—over and over and over. It's just like using a screwdriver when it's a hammer you need. Using a screwdriver for a hammer's job will get you suboptimal, or worse, no results, in addition to wasting time and creating frustration. Forcing people through a strong-arm management style (that meeting is mandatory!) to use the wrong tool to get the job done is mediocre at best, and at most, poor management of the *work*.

So now it's time to take control of the work once and for all. And you can start doing that by taking control of meetings. Take the following steps:

1. Look at every meeting that's on your calendar for the week and put it through this filter:

   a. Does the meeting have an outcome that I understand? Can I agree that the best way to achieve this outcome is through a meeting?

   b. Is my role clear?

   c. Do I know what I need to prepare so that the meeting is effective?

   If you find meetings with unclear outcomes or where you may waste time, e-mail the meeting organizer. Ask that person to be specific about the outcome, your role, and any preparation. If the organizer can't, you guessed it, respectfully decline.

2. Look at the meetings that you've scheduled for others to attend. Does your meeting invite pass the filter test? If not:

   a. Cancel the meeting.

   b. Figure out another way to get what you need when you can articulate exactly what that is—and then do it.

   c. Resend the meeting invite with the pertinent information: outcome, roles, and preparation requirements.

3. Look for recurring gatherings like staff meetings, stand-up meetings, and project update meetings. Do they pass the meeting filter test? If not, you know what to do.

4. Next time you're in a meeting that's going nowhere, do a quick mental calculation of the company's

resources that are being wasted. Then respectfully ask for clarification on what is actually needed or what the expected outcome of the meeting is.

5. Sniff out any meeting that is supposed to be a brainstorming meeting. If you've scheduled it:

   a. Cancel the meeting. Instead, send an e-mail to all participants asking them for their idea or solution on the topic you wanted to group brainstorm about. Put a deadline for when you'd like their thought, solution, or idea––for example, "Please send me your idea or solution by noon on Thursday." Ask them *not* to "Reply All." Now you have multiple suggestions that people have been able to develop and share on their own time.

   b. Next time you're in a brainstorming meeting with a bunch of people, watch what *really* happens. One or two ideas get presented initially, and everybody jumps on these. Those *must* be the best, right? That's why no "Reply All" when you're asking a group for ideas through e-mail. People see one or two ideas and then they just say, "Ditto, great idea, Sam!" without bothering to put any more thought into it.

CultureRx consulted with a company in 2008 whose CEO stated, "When I schedule a meeting, the people I invite better show up or I'll squash 'em like a bug." I guess we know who wears the pants at *that* company.

It's this style of management—that of fear and intimidation—that runs rampant in an organization whose leaders are more concerned with compliance to their rules and their need for hierarchical power than results. I wouldn't last *1 day* in that organization!

Who's with me?

Typical Questions

The following are typical questions managers ask when they're thinking about a ROWE for their team or organization. These questions are important because evolving to a ROWE requires a different way of solving common challenges. Lose no sleep! Here are the answers.

Q: Body language is important to communication. Won't messages or meanings suddenly get lost in translation?

A: What's important to communication is asking the questions you need to ask to gain clarity on what you think you don't understand. Body language, just like voice inflection, can also be misinterpreted. You're subject to misunderstanding the second something leaves your mouth, whether you're face to face or across the globe from the person with whom you're communicating. The important thing to do is focus on the outcome you need and continue to ask questions to gain the clarity and understanding for this. Relying on correct interpretation of someone's body language is a crapshoot; it doesn't guarantee effective communication.

Q: We need weekly status updates with the whole project team. What about those meetings?

A: The first question to ask yourself is, *"Why* do I need a weekly status update meeting?" Most people tell us that they spend most of the status update meeting half-listening while doing other work—until it's their turn to *report out.* If people need to read information about the project, they can do so via a shared platform. If they have a particular question about how what they read affects their piece of the project, they can go directly to the person and ask a question. Think about how you're using your resources and if the money you're spending having 20 to 30 project team members on a 2-hour call each week is appropriate (refer to meeting math). What is the outcome of the project update meeting? And is it truly the *best* way to get to the outcome?

Q: If we don't meet, how will we build effective relationships?

A: Rather than starting with how to build effective relationships, start with what everyone has in common: the work. The outcome of the work and how it's measured will require relationships to form. *How* people build relationships is based on their shared responsibility and accountability to the work—and that's up to them. Prescribing how people interact with one another—"It's important for everyone to meet face to face at least once per week to build relationships"—reinforces the belief that relationships can't be built unless there's a minimum amount of face time.

Q: What about the processes we have in place with agile that require stand-up meetings every day?

A: Take the stand-up meeting through the meeting filter:

1. What do we need exactly?
2. Is what we need relevant to the outcome we're trying to achieve or the people we're working with are trying to achieve?
3. Is having a [stand-up] the best way to get what we need?
4. Is there a more effective way to get what we need that uses everyone's time more effectively rather than a [stand-up meeting]?
5. Who is an integral part of us getting what we need?

Did you decide a stand-up meeting passes the meeting filter and is it the best way to get to your outcome? Just because there's a process in place doesn't mean you have to follow every single step if common sense tells you otherwise. Do stand-up meeting math.

Things to Try

1. Remove one recurring meeting from your calendar.
2. Ask your employees how *they* want to communicate progress on projects, rather than the

typical project update meeting where 20 people sit around a table with each person giving an update one at a time.

3. Find places on your calendar where you're double, triple, or quadruple booked. Decide which, if any, of the meetings you should or will attend using the meeting filter. Decline the others. Otherwise people will think you're attending!

4. Eliminate the drive-by meeting. Unless the building is on fire.

5. Look at any meeting that has an agenda. Is there a clear outcome? If not, ask for one *before* committing to the meeting.

Things to Avoid

1. Having more than one meeting on your calendar at any given time. After all, you can only attend *one*.

2. Putting Tentative as an attendance response. Either you're in or you're out. If you're not sure, ask questions to the meeting organizer so that you can make an intelligent decision.

3. Using your hierarchical weight to force people to come to your meeting.

4. Using the word *mandatory*. You never need to use that word. *Ever*.

(continued)

(continued)

5. Multitasking at a meeting. You know what we mean. If you need to multitask, the meeting wasn't worth your time and you're just being rude.

Get Support!

Schedule a Team Workshop. Learn more by going to www.gorowe.com/training.

Our favorite meeting-cost calculator can be found by going to www.effectivemeetings.com/diversions/meetingcost.asp.

Delighting the Customer

by Ronnie Wooten

Ronnie Wooten is the president and chief operations officer of Financial Institution Technologies, Inc., d/b/a Suntell. Founded in 1996 by bankers, Suntell has made a focused commitment to delivering integrated commercial loan risk management software solutions to the banking industry.

Suntell is located in Topeka, Kansas. The organization completed CultureRx's on-site ROWE training in August 2010. Ronnie is an active member of the ROWE Online Support Community (www.gorowe.com/community).

Once our management team had made the decision to migrate to a Results-Only Work Environment (ROWE) in 2010—and before announcing this transition to our employees—I prepared people in customer care and accounting/human resources, teams for which I have direct responsibility. We underwent a process where we identified *every single task* that each person currently performed on a daily basis, which, as you might imagine, took a lot of effort as well as a great deal of patience. The meeting lasted for what seemed to be a painfully long time, and I knew the team was completely mystified as to why I would even want them to complete this exercise. After all, I was essentially holding them "hostage" in a daylong meeting to identify all of their processes, procedures, and responsibilities—information that most of them thought that I, as the manager, should have a full understanding of. And make no mistake—I *did*. But I wanted *them* to say it

(continued)

(*continued*)

out loud and answer four questions related to each task or process so that they, too, could *see* how ineffectively we operated and how we were *not* as customer-focused as we claimed to be.

The four questions we had to answer about each task were:

1. Does this benefit our customer?
2. Does this benefit our company?
3. Does this benefit our departmental goals?
4. Does this benefit our investors?

If the answer to any of the four questions was "no," then we quickly asked a follow-up question: "Is this even necessary?" If the answer to all four questions was a solid "no," then we immediately crossed that task off the to-do list and stopped performing it altogether. We hacked away at that list for hours. As a result, we eliminated many processes and tasks that either I or previous managers had evidently created as a means to obtain value from employees who were chained to their desks by the archaic 40-hour workweek. We realized that these processes and tasks served absolutely no benefit to our customers, company, department, or investors. They were merely time fillers.

I got the old "deer in the headlights" look when I first began crossing items off the list, as if the staff could not believe I would actually remove duties. They certainly must have thought I'd lost my mind— or maybe they were amazed that I was finally seeing the light and recognizing just how ludicrous these tasks were. In some instances, the tasks were relevant and *did* serve benefit but required several people to be involved to provide the illusion of "checks and balances" along the way. For instance, three or four people would touch a new contract *before* they even contacted the new customer. Why? Couldn't we all trust the first point of contact to handle the other pieces to expedite the delivery? Wasn't the *customer* the ultimate check and balance? Wouldn't they call and complain if our delivery wasn't up to par or if we had made an error? Were we really trying to please the customer, or our corporate selves? Why not let the customer be the definitive judge of our performance? And although the team seemed leery of this idea, they embraced it and agreed to give it a whirl!

About a month after this peculiar meeting, we made the official announcement that we were going to try a new way to operate the company— ROWE—and distributed the book *Why Work Sucks and How to Fix It* to the employees. We requested they read it prior to our training workshop with CultureRx. It became quite clear to this portion of the staff when they started reading that book—and

(continued)

(*continued*)

throughout the facilitated training—why I had taken them through that task identification process previously. That's when they had their "aha!" moment. If they weren't busy filling time, they could be focusing on results and delighting our customers. And if they delighted our customers, then we would gain more referrals; and if we gained more referrals, then we could close more new sales and grow . . . and if we grew, then they could also benefit financially. They recognized that wasn't going to happen overnight; however, they held fast to their belief that if we kept at it, we would build momentum and the big wheel would pull us rather than us pushing it along.

I continue to manage the customer care group, but my role is completely different now. These individuals are truly a self-managed team. They conceive of and implement ways to delight our customers on their own—ideas that, frankly, require that they work harder and increase their own workloads. They do this voluntarily and without my needing to prod them. I'm simply there to provide coaching and mentoring as needed. They come to me only to inform me of their plans and to get one last sanity check and blessing on the idea. My response to them is typically the same: "You are doing the work. You know this customer base. I trust you." I have yet to be disappointed by granting them this level of trust. I doubt we have a single customer within our base that could come up with one negative comment related to our quality of service. In the 2 years since I passed the torch to the people doing the work, *I have not received a single complaint from a customer related to our service delivery.*

One team member brought forward a great example of how the team members come up with their own ideas for delighting the customer. This individual suggested that we hold something we call "Lunch and Learns" each month. During these gatherings, we offer a no-cost 30- to 45-minute Web-based training class to our entire customer base. The team of trainers solicits ideas from our customer base, schedules the events in advance, and notifies customers about them via e-mail campaigns. The customer attendance is astounding. We easily get attendees from more than 40 percent of our customers on a regular basis. The team has since expanded our offering to include a recording of this session on our customer portal for those who are unable to attend the live session. It's a great way to be proactive with our customer base in terms of broadening their knowledge of the system!

When we first migrated to a ROWE, our company had 30 percent more employees. We've lost them either to attrition or failure to meet results, and we did not need to replace them or fill their positions. The remaining staff came forward and

(continued)

(continued)

committed to management to pick up the workload. This would have never happened before implementing a ROWE. I'm certain that our old, larger staff believed they were overworked and at full capacity. Yet while our staff size has decreased by 30 percent, our customer base has continued to *increase*. We can do this *because* of ROWE: because our staff is focused on delighting our customers instead of on time-filling tasks.

Oh, and are our employees working 24/7? I wouldn't know, as I don't track their time. But when I talk to them, it sure sounds to me like they're embracing ROWE. They appreciate the freedom it offers and how much more balanced their lives are. I know mine is!

6

Results

Not for Every *Job?*

"**A** Results-Only Work Environment (ROWE) will never work for doctors and nurses." "ROWEs could never exist in schools." "I would never want my child care provider to be a ROWE!" Over the past 10 years, we've heard these comments umpteen times . . . and they used to make our blood boil. After all, aren't health care professionals, teachers, and child care providers all people we *want* focusing on results?!

Fortunately for our boiled blood, we can now say that ROWE *is* working in these settings. And we get to add a cherry on top: not only is ROWE *working* in the social sector, it's taking off in the public sector as well.

We won't lie; we *love* hearing skeptical comments now (in fact, we *hope* we hear them) so that we can immediately disprove them. Being able to talk about how these arenas are being positively impacted by the ROWE mind-set brings us great satisfaction. That's what we'll be sharing with you in this chapter.

When we broke off from Best Buy and started implementing ROWEs in other private sector organizations, we were sure we'd find ourselves in one office building after the other. We assumed that all of the *Dilbert*-esque workplaces across the globe would be the ones pulling ROWE in. Yet much to our surprise—and to our delight—we began hearing from educational institutions. Many of these organizations immediately saw the link between how they as an industry needed to reinvent themselves and how a ROWE could pave the path for a new trajectory.

Continuing to view education through an old mind-set wasn't going to cut it, we heard from the people who connected with us. And although this was great to hear, one entity in particular was ready to move beyond words and into action. The Prairie Lakes Area Education Agency (PLAEA) in Pocahontas, Iowa, was the (perhaps most unlikely) place in the world where the first seed for Results-Only Education would be planted.

During my first conversation with the management team, the director, Jeff Herzberg, spoke the words I hadn't heard anyone else in education say yet: "I've had it. I'm ready to blow it up." And the tone in his voice indicated he meant business. He wasn't one of those who *wanted* to blow it up but would never have the guts to actually do it; I knew he was ready to be a pioneer in his industry and lead the way for those who were just too timid. In fact, Connie Johnson, the director of marketing and communication at PLAEA, knew Herzberg wasn't kidding when she told me, "We could be known as the Pioneers in the Prairie!" And that's what they've become. In Herzberg's words, "This is the other, better way of doing education that I had been seeking for quite some time. I've felt for a while that the constraints of time and place have been negatively affecting our education setting. We've been holding kids and teachers responsible for being somewhere and not really holding them accountable for producing the right things, or at least not being certain how to measure those things. Education entities today are being held more accountable than they ever have been, so we need to figure out how to move in a direction that will align with that."

Herzberg explains:

> Before ROWE, we used to focus solely on the activities we were doing. We measured success based on how many courses PLAEA offered. Now we're looking at the *impact* of those courses. That's our measuring stick today; it's no longer good enough to just offer the activity. For example, if we're designing a literacy workshop for teachers in our area and we feel that it won't achieve the right results, we don't just put the course out there so that we can then check it off the list. We change it. Our school districts are noticing the change, too. They're already saying, "This feels like a different organization . . . we feel like somebody is finally looking at

our needs and how they can help make an impact vs. just offering X, Y, and Z."

The culture shift has been nothing short of phenomenal. For the first time in a long time, people are feeling respected for the kind of work they do. Our employees think they're working more, but they're much happier and more motivated about the work they do. In fact, we did a pre- and post-culture survey through CultureRx that involved one question concerning motivation for the work. Pre-ROWE, 51 percent of our employees responded that they were always motivated to focus on their work. Three months after ROWE training, that number had jumped to 86 percent. This gets to the heart of it. Our budget constraints pretty much guarantee that we're never going to get more people. However, we *can* change the productivity level of the people we've already got by creating a work environment they want to be part of—and by getting rid of the notion of "putting in the time." This change in motivation level, in our eyes, translates to increased productivity, which is why we think it's so very important.

We know we're on the right path. If we're going to build a system that prepares kids for the society they're going to live in, we sure need our adults to understand, experience, and really thrive in the same kind of environment. We've been expecting our educators to create this entrepreneurial spirit within kids and have done nothing to support that in terms of the education system for far too long. We've made it continually more prescriptive when, really, we need to be tearing that down.

Herzberg and PLAEA had the confidence, the desire, and the courage to be the first education entity to dive into a ROWE—and their success is apparent. Once we had our Pioneers in the Prairie, it wasn't long before the Results-Only Education ripple spread north to Intermediate School District 287 in Minnesota. In November 2011, we began working with a group of career and technical teachers to transition them to a ROWE. Tod Hoaby, construction instructor for Intermediate District (ISD) 287 on the Eden Prairie Campus of Hennepin Technical College, and Jane Holmberg, executive director of teaching and learning at ISD 287, explain the fundamental shifts in how they "do education" as a result of being in a ROWE:

> When classroom teachers hear about ROWE, they don't immediately grasp how the environment can provide much flexibility—which is understandable. Teachers have traditionally viewed their days as being highly scheduled—with the added responsibility of always needing to be present when students are in class. ROWE, however, is not first and foremost about "flexibility." Our ROWE pilot group of career and technical teachers was excited about the potential benefits of ROWE; however, the legal responsibilities of supervision loomed large.
>
> At first, the group worked around the edges of the school day. They'd leave occasionally to grade papers at a coffee shop at the end of the day or come in an hour later than usual on nonstudent days. As the group gradually got more comfortable about the fact that ROWE wasn't just about different times of

attendance but about approaching work more creatively, they were freed up to create a solution to a
perennial problem.

Because we provide services for 12 indepen-
dent school districts—and therefore, with so many
different schools—it's always tricky to create common schedules. We're most aware of the differences
in school calendars in the spring of every school
year. Schools that send students to our career and
technical courses (which are held at the campuses of
Hennepin Technical College) have varied spring
break schedules. Some always have a fixed week;
others always try to connect with Easter; and still
others change every year to accommodate a host of
other community requests. There have been years
when we've experienced four different break weeks
among the sending schools.

Before ROWE, the career and technical teachers each felt obligated to stay in his or her room,
often with very few students. They tried not to do
too much so that the students wouldn't all be in
different places in the curriculum. Of course, we
realize now that this was a great waste of student *and*
teacher time. But it took ROWE to break the cycle
of inefficiency.

Last spring, the teachers decided to use the
spring break time to help students explore courses
they would not have tried on their own. Because of
the control over time and decisions that ROWE
offers, teachers were able to gather all the students
together during spring break and rotate them

through a series of courses that exposed them to different curriculums and staff. For example, students spent Monday in the Carpentry course; Tuesday in Culinary Arts; and Wednesday in Collision Repair. This scheduling change allowed students to sample courses that they would not otherwise have attended.

There was also the added benefit for the staff. Because teachers taught their specialty only one day a week, they could devote the rest of the week to working on curriculum or other school-related needs. They could work individually or collaborate—and as many educators know, time to collaborate in most school situations is in very short supply.

We talked with the students after they'd completed the week of career exploration. Most indicated that they planned to return next year. In our minds, this change in how we're conducting teaching during spring break will positively affect our student retention rate. As students are exposed to different areas, they may latch on to something that they might not have considered.

ROWE has also helped us determine how retention is affected. For the first time, we are keeping a monthly tally of our retention rate. Beginning this school year, we will also be keeping track of the reasons students give us for why they're leaving our program.

We really feel ROWE is helping us meet student needs better, while offering a whole new level of control over time and decision making for our staff. We are working with CultureRx to implement ROWE for more groups in the upcoming school year and look forward to discovering other clear ways that ROWE changes our thinking—and allows us to do a better job.

We're hearing more and more from education entities that want to follow in PLAEA's and ISD 287's footsteps. As we think about the future of education, it's refreshing to know there are people like Jeff, Connie, Tod, and Jane out there who don't just want to skim the surface and take an easy path. Slowly but surely, an industry is revolutionizing—and this isn't something that can happen overnight. It takes place one step at a time as brave groups set examples and steer the industry onto a new course.

Jody: Pioneers of social change see the possibilities of reinvention in a whole different way. Once infused, the ROWE mind-set changes how people view the world and their communities. Removing toxic, judgmental language from the system—and giving each person the freedom to do and focus on what's right regardless of position or role—is what sets a ROWE apart from any other lame workplace program. Yup. "Flexible work options" and "Workflex" managed by managers are *not* reinvention. These kinds of programs simply reinforce the tired, old, top-down paternalistic management style

> that has frankly run its course. I just cringe whenever someone says to me, "We're flexible. We're a ROWE." ROWE is so far from a flexible work program that the two should not even be mentioned in the same sentence!

Yet another industry trailblazer hit our radar right around the time Herzberg did. Lee Ann Balta is the director of Small Blessings Childcare, a client in Indianapolis, Indiana. She connected with us because she, too, was ready to blow things up. She stated that her goal was to do the ultimate job in raising teachers who are playing a role in raising children while also providing a lot of parent education during that journey. I could immediately hear the clear connection she was making between what she does and how it's affecting society, which is a very important characteristic in any leader who moves ahead with a ROWE. It's not just about what's happening in front of your face; it's how that's transcending into the community. Balta understood this. She was also very up front with the fact that her team was getting too stuck in everyday tasks. She wanted them to feel empowered and buy in at the larger societal impact level, but she knew that she'd gone as far as she could in trying to make that happen.

Our work with Small Blessings Childcare has been so incredibly rewarding, especially since child care provider was one of the jobs people would always claim was impossible for operating in a ROWE. In the early years, people would say to us, "Well, I'd never want my child care provider to be a ROWE!" meaning, of course, that they didn't want their child care providers working off-site and leaving their children unsupervised. Seems crazy, doesn't it, now that you're this far into the content of this book? Small Blessings Childcare has now started the ripple for that industry with its success.

In Balta's words:

> ROWE has helped us to focus on *results*, which happen when we engage, practice, and reflect on researched-based practices established by the national organization to which we voluntarily submit. These practices include positive results centered on advancing children's learning and development; the qualifications, knowledge, and professional commitment of a program's teaching staff; on relevant partnerships the program establishes with both families and the community; and on the physical environment, leadership, and management that the program administration provides. These are paramount to our service industry because so many of us come from diverse and sometimes unhealthy backgrounds. They create a level playing field from which teachers and caregivers should serve all children.

> ROWE helped us see the layers of bureaucracy we created by policing one another, leading to teammates feeling discouraged, uninspired, and not at all focused on results. We also realized, through ROWE training, that we loved our checklists! What

had started out as a tool that we thought would help us had become a chain around our necks—one that limited freedom and creativity. We had created many checklists that teammates had to check, sign off on, and submit to prove they had done the work—when, in fact, we were inspecting what we inspected! We even had checklists to keep track of people who had or had not submitted their check-lists, as well as one that teachers used to complete their lesson plan process. Then we added an extra check that required neighboring teachers to review each other's lesson plans to ensure that everything on the checklist had been completed and to give feedback on their peer's lesson plan. The last straw came when we added that the teacher who created the lesson plan had to respond to the feedback of their policing peer. That's when we knew we needed ROWE. We were spiraling down a path of policing, checking, and rechecking that was eating us alive. Now, we just create lesson plans for the week and send them off to our families, giving us so much more time to focus on our results!

ROWE has also helped us understand that Sludge has no place in an environment that wants to be focused on results. CultureRx had informed us that Sludge exists in every industry—and I'd have to agree. Even in child care, we were judging how teammates were using their time—spending time judging time! Now our energy goes to making sure our families get the best of us . . . all the time. I hope that the children are hearing less Sludge in the classrooms. I want us to be modeling Results-Only practices that lead and inspire our children to collaborate, problem solve, and serve and inspire one another.

I'm convinced more than ever that our industry needs to be trained in a Results-Only environment. Our children deserve teachers and caregivers caring for them in ways that achieve results. Anything else is fraudulent and is cheating our children, families, community, and employers. Teachers and caregivers must be intrinsically focused on caring, teaching, and modeling Results-Only practices—not relying on external rewards or fear-based coercion.

Jody: I have to admit I was a bit nervous when our trainer was on-site at Small Blessings Childcare facilitating the change. Could the ROWE mind-set really take root in a *child care center?* Were we going to be able to adapt the content to deliver the change in a way that they could grab on to and run with? In the end, working with Small Blessings Childcare was a gift to us; seeing how each person's eyes would light up when realizing the true impact he or she could personally have on not only each child but the community. For example, the teachers reengineered how playground time operates after ROWE training. The new plan allows for more focused attention on smaller groups of children and fosters more interaction between age groups in other rooms. And about those pesky checklists: without certain lists, the rooms were actually *more* organized and clean than they'd ever been before! Staff members were doing what was right and were more intrinsically motivated. Even the custodian wondered, "What's going on around here?" They were one small center with the ability to see how they could pioneer a big change for the broader society. Child care providers are not changing diapers, passing out crayons, and completing checklists; they're responsible for shaping our future citizens. And that's the power of a ROWE.

Knowing that the education and child care industries are off to the races with ROWE should be, and is, comforting for many people. In many ways, these industries carry a lot of responsibility for our future as a society. Therefore, ensuring that their leadership is operating with the new model of how work can be approached is crucial to ensuring that the future unfolds with all the greatness that's possible.

Part of the challenge with this is being aware that nothing ever really stands still for very long. The health care industry knows this firsthand—and one of our clients, Lakewood Health System, not only acknowledges this but has also realized how managing in a Results-Only fashion will help them as a group meet that challenge. Tracy Hines, director of process improvement at Lakewood Health System explains:

In health care, just like with any other industry, you have to continually evaluate your market and adapt as consumers change behaviors. Innovation is part of our vision for the future, so we want to embrace new ideas and create an environment where people feel comfortable and empowered to improve our performance. This innovation may happen in daily process changes or as a big, new idea. ROWE has done both of these things for us. Once you shift to a ROWE, you unleash staff members' powerful ideas—because ROWE teaches us that it's okay to adjust and adapt as long as we're achieving the outcomes. People who have previously been conditioned to sit back and not participate in improving performance are now free to take control of their roles and improve value for their customers and themselves. Managers in a ROWE learn to embrace their employees' daily innovation, which encourages everyone to be the CEO [chief executive officer] of [his or her] job. And you can see the staff's enhanced engagement in the results.

One of the metrics Lakewood is watching is Clinic Accounts Receivable (AR) days. They began their ROWE journey in mid-April 2012 and are moving toward their goal of 28 AR days:

January 2012: 33.28
February 2012: 36
March 2012: 37.87
April 2012: 32.76

May 2012: 30.03

June 2012: 31.77

July 2012: 29.6

As Laurie Bach, vice president of hospital services at Lakewood states, "ROWE is a work culture that brings employees to the next level of motivation and performance, as it is an affirmation of trust and accountability!"

Our work with the social sector has led us to uncover a few crucial facts that tell us ROWEs will, and must, continue to spread in this arena:

1. Doing more with less in these types of settings is *necessary*—and needs to start happening *now*. Merely asking people to do more is not an option. Setting a foundation for both freedom and accountability will ensure that the people who are initiating more on their own are *doing* that much more

2. Recruiting people into social sector jobs is becoming increasingly difficult, and it's simply not realistic to offer more money than people are making in their current positions. Something must be the differentiator—and this is where a ROWE comes in.

3. Motivating staff requires that you remind people of the reason they joined the organization in the first place, not figuring out what else you can give them to *make* them deliver. People who work in the social sector are there because they are connected to their purpose—or at least they used to be. Small Blessings Childcare's Lee Ann Balta talked about how her staff

was focused on tasks and never-ending checklists. This is the rut in which many organizations find themselves, something that can be especially dangerous in the social sector. Because the potential for helping people and changing their lives for the better is so great in these positions, it's particularly alarming when you hear that employees in a school or hospital are stuck at the level of tasks, activities, and checklists. Bringing back the intrinsic motivation that attracted the employees to their roles in the first place is critical.

4. Results need a renewed focus. Every social sector organization with which we've spoken has said that they've lost their attachment to results. They've fallen into the safety net we mentioned in Chapter 4: they assume that because people are physically present and putting in time, *something* must be happening. They also admit that they're failing to deliver consequences for nonperformance. More often than not, they make up excuses for why employees don't achieve results, and they feel compelled to give second chances. Of course, a second chance might be necessary at certain times. However, if this is the norm for how the organization is running, members will never take the focus on results seriously, regardless of how many times you talk about it.

While CultureRx has been active in the social sector settings, we've also been tapped by the public sector. The drivers and the "yeah buts" in the public sector are similar to what we've discussed in earlier chapters, but there is one unique protest we often encounter. Once government agencies really get their heads around what a ROWE means (and like what the mind-set will do for them), their anxiety about public perception comes to the surface. Taxpayers, it turns out, want to know that government workers have their butts in their cubes in their office buildings from 8 AM to 5 PM Monday through Friday. They are paying for government workers to put in their *time*—period. It's funny how taxpayers complain about how government employees are "lazy" and "just sit around"—when, from our point of view, it's taxpayers themselves providing the foundation for that to continue. In our experience, government employees want to do their best work and do it in the most productive and efficient ways; they want to utilize taxpayers' dollars to their fullest potential.

So what's stopping them? Fear that those taxpayers will call them out for being at home at 11 AM on a Monday or being featured on the local news for starting work at 8:07 AM instead of 8:00 AM. We can keep blaming government workers for having a bad work ethic, or we can take responsibility ourselves, as taxpayers, for the role we're playing in prohibiting them from delivering results for us. What do we *really* expect from our public servants? A warm chair and a time card that says "40 hours worked in a week"—or benefits applications that are processed in a timely manner, license bureau lines that move along swiftly, and social workers who truly care about the outcomes of their cases? I just don't think any of us, in our right minds, are going to say "give me 40 hours—I couldn't care less if my tax dollars are producing results."

The Human Services and Public Health Department (HSPHD)[1] in Hennepin County in Minneapolis, Minnesota, has been the pioneer in helping public sector entities see the necessity in changing this perception. But they haven't done it by telling the public to alter their opinions; they're doing it by showing their results and continuing to come up with new, innovative ways to serve their customers.

Human services chief financial officer for Hennepin County Curt Haats, shares:

> While implementing ROWE in a public sector setting has presented unique challenges, it has also provided our department a source of energy in a challenging environment. The recent economic recession has put a tremendous strain on government safety net agencies. At the same time, federal and state funding for the services we provide has been declining and the ability to raise money through property taxes, our one locally controlled revenue, is challenging given the decline of the housing market.
>
> Unlike a for-profit business during a recession, we actually see the demand for our "product" (social and economic benefits) increase. However, the payers of services do not have the ability to fund the increased demand. We can meet those increased

---

[1]HSPHD consists of a number of focused but flexible service areas, common internal support systems, and cross-department integrated initiatives all working together to build better lives and stronger communities for the individuals, families, and communities of Hennepin County.

demands only through new models of service delivery.

Moving our Human Services and Public Health Department into a Results-Only Work Environment has helped unleash the creativity and energy our staff members have to address problems. One thing I have experienced is more staff are willing to ask, "Why?" And I don't just mean, "Why are we doing this?"—as a means to drive out non-value-added activities—but also, "Why *can't* we do this?" *That* is the creativity we need at all levels of an organization.

This has simply been a very demanding environment in which to deliver services. We asked an increased amount of employees to do more and had to freeze their salaries for 3 straight years at the same time. Yet our staff members are very dedicated to the department's mission. Embracing a ROWE has allowed us to engage everyone in finding new ways to work. We were able to return everyone's focus to our ultimate organizational "results" and gave each person an opportunity to have a say in how to do [his or her own job] to achieve those results. ROWE unleashed that opportunity, and that energy that has helped the department cope with the significant challenges we have faced.

Following Hennepin County's lead in county government, Wisconsin's St. Croix County quickly jumped on board with the twenty-first century way of approaching work. St. Croix is a local government agency whose mission is to promote the safety, health, and welfare of citizens through innovation and cooperation while providing services in a fiscally responsible and accessible manner. Their approximately 600 employees seek to meet citizens' needs in the following priority areas: community development, public safety and criminal justice, protection of at-risk populations, transportation, economic development, and financial health of the county.

As Tammy Funk, human resources (HR) director for the county, and Pat Thompson, county administrator, explain:

> St. Croix County originally explored the ROWE model as a possible way to reduce the need for office space, as we are faced with the need to update or expand facilities—yet as a government agency, we also need to be sure to do so in a fiscally prudent manner. We conservatively began our journey with three pilot departments to analyze the impact on employees and the public. We made a commitment that if we found that these did not have a positive impact on customer service, the ROWE pilots would be discontinued.
>
> One of the departments was concerned at the beginning that the state performance ratings not decline as a result of the pilot. Well, not only did they not decline, the state metrics showed that the high performance ratings even improved. In fact, the 6-month review of the established department metrics for all three pilots found the achievement of a number of positive objectives, including increased

job satisfaction, ability to recruit and retain high-quality staff, enhanced productivity, and a growth in customer service performance measures. Staff also report better health and client outcomes as a result of having their supervisor's trust—and being able to control their own time and focus their efforts on results. As we move to a pay-for-performance method of compensation at St. Croix County, our ROWE departments are ahead of the game; we've already established performance measures and identified specific goals and results for each team member.

ROWE is a transformational shift in mind-set. It requires supervisors and their staff to truly outline expected results and define appropriate performance measures. Employees are then held accountable for those results, not for time worked. It is no longer about making sure staff members are physically at work Monday through Friday 8–5, but rather that they are achieving their results.

These organizations have proved that they are able to operate in a ROWE and that they are committed to the future of managing performance, not people's every move. It's certainly powerful, and a bit scary, to think of social and public sector entities *not* being focused on the right things. But, sad as it is, we're confident in telling you that 90 percent of them aren't. They're doing just enough of the right things to slide by without serving children, patients, students, and taxpayers in the best possible ways. No, children in child care facilities aren't being outright *neglected*—but is that good enough? Knowing that individuals providing care are probably more worried about their checklist than they are about Sarah, who needs help washing her hands, or Tyler, who needs a few extra cuddles to fall asleep during nap time, is *not* the way it should be. Students in classrooms feel stuck and frustrated in their learning journey, instead of exhilarated and ready for more, because teachers are sticking to one path for providing education that might only fit 20 percent of their students. The rest need to just suck it up. It doesn't feel right, yet the wheel of education keeps turning in a way that's not doing society any good. Then there are nursing home residents who are spending what could be the last days of their lives receiving care from people who feel forced to be compliant with outdated rules—instead of feeling empowered to use the compassion that drew them to their jobs to actually *care* for residents in a human-to-human way. It's more important to get the cart back to the kitchen by X time than it is to stop by a room where a resident might be calling for help in reaching her water glass.

Things don't need to be this way—and we don't need to endure 20 years of "deep-dive" identification about what's wrong in these industries. We've seen with our very own eyes in a short enough amount of time how these industries' pioneers who've said, "We've had enough—let's turn this around" are succeeding. As the chief information officer of our client Fairview Health Services, Terry Carroll, has said, "ROWE is simple, but so elegant." Going back to Chapter 1, helping an industry move out of the 1950s is about taking away what doesn't make sense to pave the way for innovation, not about adding more on top of a screwed up culture.

Jody: People aren't stupid. Whenever management comes in with yet another flavor-of-the-month program that everyone knows will only last fleetingly, it reinforces that common attitude: we all just have to lay low, put in our time, and this too shall pass. It emphasizes the notion that "management knows best." I remember when we all had to remove waste from our work at Best Buy by "shooting the rattlesnakes." Really? And we wonder why people become disengaged and just want to "leave early"?

So with all of the positive change occurring in the highlighted organizations in this chapter, why aren't the social and public sectors implementing ROWEs left and right? What could possibly be holding them back? With regard to the social sector, there are definitely forces that can feel out of organizations' control that cause the big red light to blink "Danger!" We often hear the excuse that, "We have regulations imposed on us by X, Y, and Z, and if we don't follow them, we'll be subject to serious consequences. Did we mention *serious*? A ROWE might put us at risk for not following the regulations the way we should." We've found that a common phrase is often used as a crutch throughout the organization where medical, financial, or safety regulations exist. In response to, "Why do you do it that way?" we hear, "We have to; it's a *regulation.*" It's a phrase that shuts people up—and one that also impedes innovation. It's easier to say, "It's a regulation," than to stop and *really* ask, "Why *do* I do it this way?" We've uncovered that the umbrella of regulations in the health care and education industries can also cause some phantom "rules" to surface based on regulations. In other words, employees start to think they can never change the way *anything* is done because it's set up that way to comply with regulations. Tod Hoaby from Intermediate School District 287 shares these two examples:

1. The basic work year for employees states that "it shall be one hundred eighty-three (183) days falling between August 20 and June 15. Within the basic work year there shall be one hundred seventy-five (175) student contact days and eight (8) non-student contact days, one (1) of which may be used as a professional leave day. Individual staff cannot work more than two hundred forty (240) days per contract year."

   "This paragraph obviously cites the length of the school year and how much student contact we should have," Hoaby explains. "In order to get the results that I want or need in my job in a ROWE, I may have to do things differently—for instance, have more student contact—On the reverse side, I may need *less* student contact or less time working in order to reach my goals or get the results I am shooting for. I have found that I do not mind answering e-mails or going to a meeting in the summer like I used to because I have found that all of this ties in with meeting or getting the results I want."

2. "For Salaried Employees: Within the eight (8) hour work day there shall be no more than six (6) hours of student contact or 30 hours of student contact averaged throughout the work week. In addition, there shall be one (1) hour of daily prep time which may be split into two (2) segments and a one-half (1/2) hour duty-free lunch. The remainder of the work day shall be for other professional activities."

Hoaby explains, "In this paragraph, the work day becomes very rigid. That is not how ROWE works for us. Yes, we do have to be in the classroom when the students are here for our courses. But in a ROWE, we realize that there are other ways that teaching and learning can happen. Maybe students learn better at 5:00 PM or 7:00 PM rather than the traditional 7:30 AM to 3:00 PM time slot.

"We've also found that we can have prep time anywhere, at any time. Or we can eat lunch whenever, wherever we want. Neither of these needs to fall within the 8-hour workday. When our 'required' student contact time is done, we have the freedom to go anywhere we want to fulfill not only the rest of the contract, but to meet *our* results as well. The only thing limiting us at this time is the traditional time slots or classroom times when students are in school. We need a major paradigm shift to truly become great educators."

The biggest hurdle in the public sector, one that's probably connected with the public perception cited earlier, is the belief that a new administration will bring a new way of doing things. So why spend the energy transitioning to a ROWE when the next person (or group of people) in the office will just take it away? Now, we ask the you, enlightened readers of this book, Can someone take a ROWE away? Please shake your head from right to left. Do it again just for good measure.

But *have* public sector leaders *tried* to take ROWEs away? Sadly, yes. The ROWE pilot for the US Office of Personnel Management (OPM) yielded typical results. Data from the pre- and post-surveys we conducted as part of the training process indicated a significant increase in employee satisfaction during the early transition period. There was also a noteworthy cultural change that showed both employees and managers exhibiting behaviors focused on specific results they needed to achieve rather than hours worked. As a result of the ROWE training process, managers and employees began working together to create the necessary standards and processes to most effectively achieve and measure results. The post-survey also indicated that employees perceived leadership as generally more proactive versus reactive, priorities as clearer versus lacking direction, and reinforcement as more consistent. All good things, right? Things upon which we'd *hope* our government would build. After all, what is any administration—on either side of the fence—always touting? *Results.*

However, OPM didn't have the guts we know are needed to continue the evolution toward a true ROWE. As Director John Berry stated in the *Federal Times*, "employees' goals—which were a crucial element for ROWE to succeed—weren't set clearly enough, and the metrics used to hold employees accountable for getting their work done were also lacking. Communication between employees and managers also was not clear . . . we tried it, and we gave it a good run. We've wrapped up the pilot, essentially, so we're not doing it anymore."

Any organization, public or private, that transitions to a ROWE will uncover some painful information that causes discomfort. OPM's problem was that their goals weren't as clear as they should be, their metrics weren't easily identifiable, and their communication was not understandable. Other organizations might see these areas as *opportunities*, not showstoppers. After all, one of ROWE's many goals is to expose the truth (which can sometimes be ugly). Leaders who can accept reality for what it is will guide their organization through the challenges to successfully come out the other side. Leadership in a ROWE, especially in the public sector, must be strong.

To be fair, OPM had a big spotlight on them during their ROWE pilot and felt the heat of that in a way that most organizations don't. They were faced with a choice: continue through the discomfort, come out the other side, and experience positive consequences that no administration can deny, or call it quits because it's just too hard.

This is a decision that other public sector entities may need to make in the face of political winds that are always changing. It's our hope, for this country, that the right decision will be made in the future.

The move to a ROWE is inevitable for all organizations. The excuse, "We can't be a ROWE because we're public sector" or "There's no way we can go to a ROWE because we need to *be here* for our work" or "A ROWE won't to tight work for us because we're so incredibly customer-centric" are all cop-outs—and just ways to say, "We're too scared to focus on results because we don't know how."

The clients we work with in both the public and private sectors have been the organizations that have been humble and courageous enough to say, "We *can* improve." Some are in a very challenging place when their transition to a ROWE begins, and some are at the top of their game. Regardless of the scenario, these organizations know it's best to ensure that a Results-Only (not a results-*oriented*) foundation exists as the future unfolds.

Pretending you're immune from needing to focus on and manage results doesn't do anyone any favors . . . well, except maybe your competition.

Things to Try

1. Be a pioneer; *every* job in *every* industry can be Results-Only.
2. Eliminate unnecessary checklists. And yes, some *are* unnecessary.

3. Look at your industry regulations. Now ferret out the phantom rules that have surfaced. Do you need them?

4. Focus on efficiency versus "more resources." Chances are, you're being careful with budget, so don't waste it.

5. Listen to what your employees *really* want and believe that they can and will produce results that satisfy customers and communities.

Things to Avoid

1. Gnashing your teeth about flexibility. You've read the book now. Foundationally, you know you're using the wrong platform.

2. Using money as the carrot to lure people into the industry. You know now that it's not what really motivates them in the long run.

3. Being a roadblock to process change. Why would you get in the way of change that's safe, legal, and cost-neutral?

4. Calling it quits with ROWE. Address performance and goal setting; don't take away the foundation that's actually focusing on the *right* thing.

5. Saying, "We're never going to a ROWE here." This translates to, "We've never going to focus on results here." And this isn't something

(continued)

(continued)

that your employees *or* your customers will receive well.

Get Support!

Visit www.gorowe.com/training to learn more about the Go Beyond Telework Worskhop for Teams.

Results-Only Competency-Based Education

by Jeff Herzberg

Jeff Herzberg is the chief administrator of Prairie Lakes Area Education Agency (PLAEA).

Located in Pocahontas, Iowa, PLAEA's mission is to ensure success for all learners through collaborative partnerships. The organization serves 14 counties across 8,000 square miles that includes 44 public school districts and 11 accredited nonpublic schools, which are composed of 30,000 students and 3,500 educators.

Herzberg's leadership team experienced CultureRx's on-site Leadership Summit in January 2011 and went on to establish a ROWE pilot through CultureRx's on-site ROWE workshop in August 2011, and proceeded with having CultureRx certify internal PLAEA trainers to bring ROWE forward to the rest of the agency.

The Carnegie Unit. For years, this has been the foundation of the education system in the United States, and it goes like this: sit in class for a specific amount of time and number of days. When the bell rings, get up and go to another class for the same amount of time and number of days. If you sit through these classes of predetermined lengths and earn a passing grade, you advance to the next level. Essentially, this system was created to prepare students to work in factory-style work environments that were also based on time and tasks designed to fit into an assembly line system.

We have known for some time that this system has not served many of our students very well. Rather, it has left many of our special education students, gifted and talented students, English language

(*continued*)

(continued)

learners, and low socioeconomic status students feeling like round pegs trying to fit into our educational system's square holes. Even students who have done well "playing the game of school" are kept from reaching their full potential by this factory-style environment.

Creativity, innovation, critical thinking, and problem solving have often given way to predetermined semester lengths, timed standardized tests, and prescriptive lessons that have had to fit into 45-minute time increments. Students were traditionally judged and graded based on the *amount of time* it took to do something, not *whether they knew how* to do the work. Handing in work late resulted in lower grades, and students were sometimes required to stay after school to finish it. Students who were able to do the work at a quicker pace typically received additional work, and problems like boredom and behavior issues often reared their heads.

But as change is brewing in the twenty-first century workplace, change is also brewing to address this mismatch between the new workplace and the school environment that is supposed to be preparing students for life after high school. This new approach to education is called competency-based (or proficiency-based) education. States around the country are working to implement a system that meets today's student needs of personalization and passion-filled learning.

There are obvious parallels between competency-based education and a Results-Only Work Environment (ROWE). Students of competency-based education advance to the next levels by demonstrating that they've mastered the required competencies (results). Time is no longer a driver of learning. What matters is mastery of a competency, not the amount of time it takes to learn it.

As a result of this new approach, students in some schools across the country have been able to obtain their learning outside the four walls of the classroom and outside the normal hours of the school day. For example, a student in New Hampshire can take a summer course at the Seacoast Science Center in Rye. That student can then demonstrate the science competencies back at his local high school and earn credit if he achieves at the mastery level. Students are finally able to take the amount of time *they need* to learn at the mastery level, instead of having to fit into the old system of "one size fits all." Results are clearly defined for students; they know exactly what they need to do and are not hindered by previously used, incompatible time requirements.

Our students are moving toward a results-oriented system, so isn't it time that our educational workplaces did the same? After all, if we expect our teachers and administrators to educate students within a competency-based system, doesn't it make

(continued)

(continued)

sense that we should create a ROWE for the adults who work in the system? We know that our educators already work many hours outside the traditional school day to find ways to improve the learning environment in their classrooms. Educators are accountable to ensure each student learns. This is their bottom line, or if you will, their result.

A ROWE in education provides for a workplace that honors the profession and allows adults the freedom to meet students' needs while helping them achieve high-level results. Our students *and* adults need to be able to create, innovate, think critically, and solve problems—all of which can be very difficult to do within the confines of our current education system.

Can you imagine an educational system in which the adults in the system make the ROWE guideposts come alive? People at all levels would stop doing any activity that is a waste of their own time, the school's time, or the school's money. Work isn't a place you go; rather it's something you do. Nobody talks about how many hours they work or feels guilty, overworked, or stressed out—and no one judges anyone else about how they spend their time.

This is just what has begun to happen at Prairie Lakes Area Education Agency (PLAEA) in northwest Iowa. With the help of CultureRx, PLAEA operated a pilot project during the 2011–2012 school year to see how a ROWE in education would operate. A few other factors played into this decision, one of which was shrinking resources, both financially and in regard to personnel. The area covers more than 8,000 square miles—we have 230 staff members—50 fewer than we had 3 years ago. Another element was the state's desire to move toward a competency-based system.

Our pilot involved 50 people who received a 1-day immersion in ROWE by CultureRX. They embarked on a journey that will change the face of the agency, and hopefully education, forever.

Each of those teams at PLAEA became very focused on results—a mind-set that's made a tremendous difference in our work. Staff report being more satisfied and more productive with their work, as they're able to bring a laser-like focus to improving the learning outcomes of all the children and students we serve.

Operating with this new mind-set has created a clash between the new versus old way of "doing education." The clash stems from the collision of the old educational system, which was designed to sort and select our students into thinkers and doers, to the new system, in which we need everybody to think and do. Competency-based education and ROWE are a great match to help all students think critically, problem solve, and become more

(continued)

(continued)

responsible for their learning. It also serves to make educators responsible for their work and their impact on the next generation of leaders. We cannot continue to support passive, adult-centered learning in our school systems, because the world that awaits our young people nowadays is vastly different than it once was. Students *and* adults need to be engaged and active participants in the work they do—and we can accomplish this in competency-based education and our ROWE.

As we move forward with expansion of ROWE to the entire agency now that CultureRx has certified our PLAEA internal trainers, we believe that focusing on results ensures that the children we serve receive what they need to be successful. We are less focused on time now as we know it is the results that matter. We are trying to block out the noise and clutter of all the things we used to ask people to do that did not lead to improved results for our students. We are moving to an environment in which we make all meetings optional; we do not require people to update their calendars on a daily basis (they still keep one for themselves, because they know where they need to be to achieve their results) but rather focus on the work that needs to be done. And we are trying to involve more of our staff members in our agency's leadership. We hope that the people closest to the decision impact will embrace this enhanced autonomy and decision-making authority, because we know that this will lead to a more effective and enjoyable work environment.

We are really trying to help the people we support to understand that accessibility, not visibility, is the key here. We are always working toward the results that are expected of us; to this end, we are making sure that we're using technology—things such as Skype, Google Hangouts, and TurboMeeting—to eliminate the miles and time spent away from the actual work of serving kids, families, and educators. We are not standing around schools and waiting for someone who might need help; rather, we promote our accessibility by cell phones, Google voice phone contact, and e-mail at all times. In doing so, we know that our staff are going to be working outside the normal 8:00 to 4:30 time frame—and we want to validate this by encouraging them to be in charge of their schedule to achieve the expected (and in some cases mandated by state and federal government) results. They do not need permission to leave at 3:30 to get to their son's piano recital or daughter's volleyball game. They will be judged on results, not on being somewhere . . . we expect them to make a contribution and to eliminate presenteeism wherever it exists.

ROWE in the Public Sector

by Nancy Dietl Griffin

Nancy Dietl Griffin is the director of human resources (HR) for the Minnesota Judicial Branch.

The Human Resources Division of the Minnesota court system serves as a partner with Minnesota Judicial Branch leadership in developing policies and programs, providing HR services that enable people to achieve the strategic priorities of the branch, and in creating an innovative and proactive organization where employees and judges are valued and the public is well served.

The Minnesota Court System began their on-site CultureRx training in September 2011.

Similar to many human resources (HR) professionals, I like to keep abreast of innovations in human capital management. Over the past few years, I had read articles in *Fortune* magazine, the local newspaper, and the like, describing the Results-Only Work Environment (ROWE) "movement" that had started at Best Buy. I read it all with particular interest, as the retailer's world headquarters is located blocks from where I grew up. The idea that this paradigm shift had its inception in my backyard piqued my interest. I thought at the time (in 2008), "How cool to work whenever I want, wherever I want. Too bad that would never fly in my hierarchical, conservative, public sector organization." Although the concept clearly resonated with me, I could not see how it would ever work within my organization and its deeply ingrained culture. Despite being one of the most innovative and well-regarded state agencies in the country, my initial impression was that a ROWE simply wasn't for us. I felt it was a concept for those technology firms whose very DNA is predisposed to flexibility, freedom, creativity, and rapid pace—not exactly the descriptions that come to mind when describing the public sector.

The next few years were not easy. The Great Recession posed enormous challenges to all organizations, whether publicly held, private, not-for-profit, or government. With billion-dollar state budget deficits, funding cuts, and multiyear salary and hiring freezes, many of us public sector HR professionals found ourselves immersed in a world of contingency planning, reductions in workforce, reorganization, and the need to do more and more with fewer and fewer resources. It is easy to see how my interest in a ROWE got crowded out in this mode of scarcity, risk aversion, and hunkering down.

After a few years, our HR management team, along with members of our labor management committee, began to notice the toll that living this way was taking on employee morale. In the beginning of the recession, our employees were simply happy to have jobs. They watched neighbors and loved ones who were laid off experience struggles with long-term unemployment, and this realization and gratitude sustained them—initially. But years of having to do an increasing amount of work with a

(continued)

(continued)

shrinking staff began to take their toll. With the demands of constant organizational change—and the public's increasing expectations to provide improved services—staff members began to lose their resiliency. The *Economist* article "Over-stretched"[1] referred to the Great Recession as the perfect storm for employee disengagement. Our HR management team began to take a deeper look at morale issues, and it became clear that we would be headed toward serious employee disengagement if we did not address emerging staff concerns.

In many ways, it took hitting bottom of the Great Recession and resulting impact to compel our organization to take a hard look at our culture. We considered both our strengths and challenges as we became more open to solutions we would not have considered in the past. Despite the many drawbacks of organizational crisis, it *does* force change—and in our case, prompted us to examine the benefits that implementing a ROWE would bring.

After doing some research, our HR management team had identified a number of potential organizational risks associated with the morale issues: retaining our valued employees, attracting the best talent, improving productivity, and most of all,

[1]"Overstretched," *Economist*, Vol. 395, May 22, 2010, p. 72.

maintaining a highly engaged workforce to deliver upon our most ambitious organizational goal to date: transforming to a paperless e-government agency within 3 years. Moreover, we identified a future that used technology to serve the public across traditional boundaries. Staff in one part of the organization (or working remotely) could process work for another location, regardless of where the work originated. Similarly, we envisioned the need to provide services to the public on a 24/7 basis. The need to prepare for the future of work, as well as our ability to attract employees from the Millennial/Generation Y age group, was rapidly approaching. We knew from our existing experience that the Millennial generation works very differently than previous generations had and that our hierarchical structure was not likely to engage or retain these staff members over the long haul.

Our HR managers used employee satisfaction survey metrics to identify our strengths, primarily that our employees are proud of the work they do, feel connected to the organization's mission, and believe they can rely on their coworkers. Similarly, surveys and exit interviews reinforced our assessment that we needed to address morale. Employees increasingly reported feeling overwhelmed, unable to keep up with their work, and weary of constant change. The mandate to do more with less was growing old. In our team's research on the best

(*continued*)

(continued)

practices that promote employee engagement, we relied on the latest research from Gallup, the Human Capital Institute, and Dr. Theresa Welbourne[2] from the University of Southern California's Center on Organizational Effectiveness. We formed our own hypothesis that a combination of both employee empowerment and accountability, in an environment of communication, feedback, and recognition, led to engagement. We simplified the formula as

Empowerment + accountability = engagement

The challenge, then, was to find a framework to embed these in our culture.

This was the backdrop for my fortuitous meeting with CultureRx. I explained to Cali in great detail the engagement challenges our HR team had identified while Cali listened intently. I explained the ambitious set of organizational strategic priorities ahead and emphasized that we needed every employee to be engaged to meet these goals. I felt both overwhelmed and relieved that Cali understood our predicament, as she explained that she was very confident that a ROWE was the vehicle to address our challenges.

[2]Theresa M., Welbourne, "From the War for Talent to the Battle for Future Heroes: The Story of the Recession's Neglected Warriors and How to Make Sure They Are Not Poached Away," 2010, www.leadershippulse.com.

I had so many questions in that initial meeting. How could staff who must serve the public at our counters possibly work from anywhere, let alone any*time?* Surely, administrative support staff who report to executives would need to be in the office every day from 8 to 5. There must be staff like these who cannot work in a ROWE. Cali asked me, "Is there anyone in your organization who does not have results to achieve at work? A ROWE is about results. As long as you can focus on results, you can be in a ROWE."

Something broke loose when she said that. At that moment, I began to see how a ROWE—with its intense focus on results—was exactly the vehicle we needed for achieving accountability. Similarly, the corresponding freedom of "Do whatever you want whenever you want to reach your results" would serve as the empowerment we needed to ignite staff engagement.

Suddenly, it all became crystal clear. In a time when public sector organizations are facing intense scrutiny to deliver services to the public in the most effective and efficient ways possible, how could we *not* do everything in our power to promote workplaces that focus intensely on *results?* Members of the public increasingly expect government to provide services on par with our society as a whole. This means providing instant access to information, conducting routine business such as fee payment

(continued)

(continued)

over the Internet, and ensuring high-quality customer service. To meet these expectations, our agency needed to retain our valued staff as the economy rebounded, compete for top talent as other organizations would begin to increase compensation, and motivate our staff—now more than ever. I realized that it was only through our *human* talent that we would be able to achieve our ambitious goals.

At that point, I knew *I* was convinced about a ROWE. The next challenge was to persuade our organizational leadership to take a leap. I spent the next few months strategizing about how to make the concept a reality. Taking the following steps was crucial to convincing senior management to put their faith in me and my belief in a ROWE:

1. **Identify champions and be strategic.** Choose a combination of senior-level, operational, and HR managers. Select credible visionary leaders who can influence their leaders, peers, and direct reports. Educate them about a ROWE and enlist them in selling the shift in thinking that is needed to implement this kind of workplace.
2. **Launch pilots.** Consider introducing a few pilots throughout if your organization is too large to implement simultaneously. Another benefit to this is that pilots often do not

sound as threatening in risk-averse public sector organizations. Be sure to choose high-performing departments with strong leaders for the pilots.

3. **Offer training and support.** CultureRx provided essential orientation and support from the very beginning. The on-site training workshops conducted for our teams, along with the culture survey data that CultureRx collected, provided invaluable knowledge for us to successfully place ourselves on this new trajectory. This company lives and breathes results and regards every client's success as its own.

4. **Create documented ROWE Results Worksheets for all employees in a ROWE.** We did not want this to be prescriptive; however, because ROWE is all about results—and we wanted to increase accountability—we required all participants to have documented results. The results vary by division, and staff own their results. They draft them but managers have final approval.

5. **Network with other ROWE organizations.** Cali connected us with other public sector organizations from whom we've learned along the way. We share tips and resources for success. Because the public sector has a number of unique concerns, these resources help us navigate.

(continued)

(continued)

6. **Change is biggest for managers; support them.** It became abundantly clear from the beginning that managing in a ROWE was very different than it had been prior. Staff were excited and ready to jump in, which made sense; if they were doing their jobs and meeting their goals already, working in a ROWE brought them newfound flexibility. However, *managing* in a ROWE means coaching and holding staff accountable, skills that many managers may not have had the chance to develop. Therefore, we instituted biweekly (which eventually became monthly) ROWE manager meetings where we discussed the challenges and successes we were experiencing. The early meetings were characterized by a lot of debate about how the ROWE guideposts translated to our organization. Some managers were uncomfortable with the loss of "control" over staff schedules and seeing their employees in the office. They wanted to know how they would know if staff were being productive. Other managers shared their perspectives that if goals and results are clear and progress is tracked using the new ROWE results tools we had developed, it would become clear whether staff were not performing, an issue we could address using the tools.

7. **Address ROWE misperceptions.** Early on, we heard many staff say, "I work at a public counter; therefore, I can't work from home and I can't be in a ROWE" or "I perform administrative support work (copies, meeting coordination), so how can I be in a ROWE?" On the management side, we heard, "How will I know if my staff are working if I can't see them?" and "No one will go to meetings anymore." It is amazing how even 12 months into our ROWE culture change, some employees still make these statements. This is evidence of just how much communication and intention is involved in implementing and sustaining culture change.

8. **Before implementing a ROWE, identify the results you hope to achieve with the culture change.** This may be strong morale, reduced turnover, reduced absenteeism, and so on. Whatever it is, agree on how you will measure and report results. It is tempting to skip this when we have so many demands and are eager to implement a ROWE immediately. However, if you take the time to identify the overall results and measures for your organization, you will be in a better position to show organizational leaders—who may change as elected officials change—ROWE's successes. It's also important to be able to demonstrate how improved employee focus on results is leading

(continued)

(continued)

to improved service to the public and prudent use of public resources. Sound measures and program evaluation plans are essential to answering these critical questions.

9. **Always keep the public accountability in mind.** Private organizations do have more flexibility to work various hours in a workweek to achieve results. On the other hand, exempt employees in most private sector organizations receive their full salary regardless of whether they work 12 or 62 hours in a pay period. Exempt employees in the public sector also are expected to put in the hours required to perform the job, which often means long hours, just like in the private sector. However, we do have obligations to work the full complement of hours the public is paying us for over the course of a pay period.

Based on our ROWE experience, I firmly believe that billion-dollar revenue deficits and double-digit funding cuts can be the impetus for rapid innovation and efficiencies in proactive public sector organizations—transformations that would have taken years to implement in a status quo funding era. When it is a matter of survival, well-led public sector organizations are prompted to examine all aspects of operation, including long-held assumptions about where and how employees should get work done. I like to think we would have come to a ROWE even if we did not have severe funding shortfalls and workforce reductions as precipitating events. Regardless, any public sector organization that believes that results are critical to achieving the organization's mission and strategic priorities; that providing efficient and innovative service to the public and prudent and transparent use of resources are nonnegotiable; and that engaged employees who are held accountable for achieving well-thought-out goals are crucial to achieving these ambitious goals *cannot afford* to ignore the changes that are happening all around us. We in the public sector must take proactive measures to increase employee engagement and create workplaces that treat employees as adults with the freedom to work the way they want to work. This will position us to attract and retain a new generation of workers, and it will align with a future that uses technology to serve the public in innovative ways.

Epilogue

We hope that as you've read this book, you've had a feeling stirring inside you that you may not have felt before. If you're a manager, it might have felt like your stomach was sinking during the first few chapters, like you feel during the first part of a roller coaster drop after you've eaten a big lunch with an even bigger dessert. But hopefully by now, you're feeling like you're on firm ground again, and any nausea you may have had is subsiding. Most of all, we hope you're spurred to take action, to change some of the ways you've been operating just because "that's the way they've been done" for decades. If you're an employee—*anywhere*—you might feel like there's a big present in front of you that you may or may not be able to open. Some of you may feel frustration; others might experience indescribable excitement. No matter what the feeling, these pages hold the promise of what this rising age of "management" will set in motion for you: finally, an opportunity to use your adult brains to do what's best for your work— and your *life*—every single day.

There *is* something that no one who reads this book will be able to deny, regardless of position in an organization: the deep societal impact that will occur once this age of management comes on full force. As we first started moving a Results-Only Work Environment (ROWE) across Best Buy headquarters, and even into our first subsequent client sites, we'd often hear, "Who do you think you are? You're telling us about this utopia of a work environment—what are you going to go after next? World peace?" The funny thing was that we never really answered that question. In our minds, there's no end to what the ROWE mind-set, when operating in brain after brain, organization after organization, country after country, can influence. We're not trying to be arrogant, but we've seen this ripple effect start to take hold. And as it gets bigger, it will be an amazing force that will be visible to everyone, everywhere.

What might it look like? Here's a glimpse:

According to the Families and Work Institute, 50 percent of US workers feel overwhelmed by a growing number of job tasks and longer hours. This isn't getting better; it's just getting more and more dismal. Organizations are desperately trying to do more with less, and as they project this mantra from on high, people are forced to sprint nonstop on a treadmill that has no off switch.

Now . . . try this on for size: *in a ROWE, people at all levels stop doing any activity that is a waste of their time, the customer's time, or the organization's money.* Managers place the power in employees' hands and enable them to make commonsense decisions based on their outcomes and associated measures. People automatically edit their work and remove low-priority tasks. Most organizations are already trying to do this, and some succeed. Unfortunately, and this is the very important point, this editing behavior doesn't sustain. In 90 percent of the culture assessments we conduct, organizations tell us that when processes are improved or waste is removed, managers immediately fill that space by giving more work. As we discussed in Chapter 2, this undermines employees' desire to make efficient decisions for their organizations. They're stuck between a rock and a hard place: they can be efficient and then be punished with more work (leading to feeling more and more overwhelmed) or continue doing what doesn't make sense and experience Spastic Colon Sunday week after week after week. Every day, organizations are digging themselves deeper and deeper into the stress hole, not realizing how difficult it will be to dig themselves out as time marches forward.

Adding to the stress levels is the fact that 59 percent of women and 38 percent of men in the United States report having no flexibility in determining their day's start and end times (mothersandmore.org). One of the ramifications of this trend is children sitting in elementary, middle, and high school hallways hours before school begins. How ridiculous is it that parents who will be marked tardy by their control freak bosses are forced to drop their kids at school at 6 AM so they can sit in traffic for 2 hours and walk in "on time"? As a result, these children are spending precious hours where they could be sleeping—or, heaven forbid, eating a nutritious breakfast—sitting in hallways, eating a Pop-Tart from the vending machine until their classes start.

In a ROWE, employees have the freedom to work any way they want. Not just on Mondays and not just some people. *Every* person, *every* day. Children of parents who work in a ROWE have made comments like, "I never thought I'd ever get to have breakfast with you on a Wednesday!" and "None of my friends' parents get to walk them to the bus stop. I'm glad *you* can." These seem like such simple things, but they can make lasting memories in a child's eyes and get their days—and *lives*—off to a great start.

And as if the morning hours weren't bad enough, there's also the issue on the other side of the day. From 3 PM to 6 PM on weekdays, children are most likely to become victims of a crime, accident, or engage in risky behavior or commit crimes themselves. Statistics like this don't need to torture us, and we don't need expensive, time-consuming think tanks to figure out how to prevent this behavior during the late afternoon hours. We have millions of parents sitting around office buildings trying to look busy while they worry about their kids, watch their phones for text messages, and plan the best route to get home while trying to avoid the multicar pileups they can see forming from their windows. Give them all the freedom to work any way they want, and the whole scenario changes.

It's no secret that lacking control over how, when, and where work happens causes great amounts of stress. According to the American Psychological Association, 69 percent of employees report that work is a significant source of stress and 41 percent say they typically feel tense or stressed out during the workday. It's also been reported that 51 percent of employees are less productive at work as a result of stress. These statistics aren't going to turn *themselves* around, and no amount of time management or "how to reduce stress" training will have an impact. To shake things up, to make people stop to think, "What would *that* be like?" the state we're in requires one phrase: *Every day* feels *like Saturday*. This phrase, when put into practice in organizations around the country, is stirring things up. It's meant to awaken the sense of control that exists on that one day of the week where things get done, and *we* are deciding how and when that happens. Saturday is our chance to consider everything we need to get done and create our plan of attack. The plan doesn't depend on whether our boss is going to see us somewhere for a certain number of hours or how busy we appear to be while we're accomplishing our Saturday stuff. We just do it, and usually with enough time to do something enjoyable afterward.

And, of course, there's the change in commuting behavior that will occur all over the world when everyone starts hearing—really hearing—the guidepost we've been screaming for the past several years: *work isn't a place you go; it's something you do*. We've heard it over and over from parties who want to sound like they're doing something futuristic. In reality, there's really only a small percentage of people and organizations who understand the depth of what this truly means. The rest are still sitting in an abyss made up of:

- Space that denotes a *certain status*. The larger the building, the more beautiful the architecture, the greater the amount of on-site amenities must all equal a fantastic place to work and an excellent place to do business with. Then there's the whole matter of the office/cubicle hierarchy, the size and location of one's office (window or not?). Don't even get us started.

- The *allocation of a "spot"* to each employee.
- Beliefs about how, when, and where work should happen that continue to fuel the rise of more office buildings.

As we discussed in Chapter 1, this notion of work being something you do versus a place you go comes to life when you realize that a *place* does not define the work or prove that the right work is even being done. No matter what the job or what the organization exists to do, the mind-set of work being something everyone *does* will start to take hold.

Another important societal impact that will surface as this mind-set changes is the level of *inclusion* that organizations around the world will start to experience. We must recognize the limits we're placing on our organizations, on what we could be producing, on the talent we could be using and acknowledge that these are all self-imposed. It's just not enough for *inclusion* to be the happy word thrown around corporate town where 20 percent feel included and the other 80 percent feel—and are being treated like—crap.

For example, other than the cost of health insurance, the number 1 impediment to employing folks with disabilities in the knowledge economy is the lack of affordable, accessible transportation to the work site. "Of the nearly 2 million people with disabilities who never leave their homes, 560,000 never leave home because of transportation difficulties," states the "Equity in Transportation for People with Disabilities" report by the American Association of People with Disabilities and the Leadership Conference Education Fund. Now we know that it's necessary to be in a certain place to reach certain outcomes for some jobs. But for others, especially knowledge-type work done by the likes of software engineers, architects, and marketing professionals, there is absolutely *no need* to be in a specific place. Imagine how many more people we could include in our organizations if we weren't worried about relocating them or making sure they show their face just to fulfill an outdated requirement that we *think* means something.

If, however, you're still locked into the thinking that work must, under any circumstances, be treated as someplace we *go*, then let's discuss it in health terms. A study conducted in Dallas, Fort Worth, and Austin, Texas, found that the longer your daily commute, the more likely you are to have high blood pressure, an oversized waistline, and other health problems that increase your risk for chronic disease. It's not a huge revelation that sitting in a car for hours every week— *under* and heading *into* stressful circumstances—will cause health problems. What *is* surprising is that the study's lead author, Christine Hoehner, assistant professor of public health sciences at Washington University in St. Louis, made this statement: "You can't change your commute, or the fact that you are at a desk all day. Driving to work has long been a part of everyday life. Daily walks can be as well." Now that's what I call major encouragement! This is a prime example of how and why we're stuck. Someone like Hoehner, whose job it is to work to improve people's health, has essentially said: "Just keep commuting, and sitting at your desk all day whether you have to or not—but add in a walk here and there." Seems to me that our public health sciences professionals should be using data from their studies to make the case that we need to change, not just continue carrying on as we always have.

If you're wondering whether you're one of those who might fall into this category of still being stuck in the abyss of thinking of work as somewhere you go, here are some signs:

- You find yourself saying, "The capacity of this building is 500 people, and we're almost there. Let's get cracking on finding a new site."
- You think, "The vice president of that department is moving to the eighth floor. How soon can we get her team moved up there?"
- You wonder, "What is Alison up to? Haven't seen her for over a week!"
- You tell a new hire, "We all show up around 8 AM; we'll see you then!"

Our guess is that if you're still stuck, you may still be monitoring the comings and goings of employees around you. You take zealous notice of who is coming in "late," who is leaving "early," and who has used the greatest number of sick days. And you can't help it; all of this costs organizations money, right? The "MetLife Caregiving Costs Study: Productivity Losses to U.S. Businesses" states that "Absenteeism, reported by the majority of caregiving employees, costs $5 billion, while partial absenteeism, affecting virtually all working caregivers, accounts for nearly $2 billion in losses. Add workday interruptions, which account for at least one hour a week per caregiver, and you have $6.3 billion more." At first glance, these statistics seem outrageous, and our gut reaction to them might be to clamp down even harder on employees being on time, putting in their hours, and giving good enough reasons for wanting take time off or use sick time. After all, that's a lot of money!

However, we must remember that there is no late and no early in the future of work; there is only achieving results. Absenteeism doesn't exist in the future; the only thing you can be absent from is the work, in which case you have a performance issue. Keeping the thoughts of the future in mind, then, we can say with confidence that the $13.3 billion statistics are a crock. Researchers arrived at them according to parameters of having hours and being in one physical place during certain periods of time. When caregivers have clear expectations, know how they're being measured, and don't have to worry about their comings and goings, productivity will go *up*—and we won't have to live in this state of thinking we're losing billions of dollars each year because of *those* people who are causing us issues.

Some of you might be thinking as you're reading, "What we're talking about here is *culture* change!" Why yes, yes we are. It doesn't matter how many times we say this during training sessions with teams to make sure they understand the depth of the journey upon which they're embarking; toward the end of our time with them, there are always participants who make that comment.

The fact is that we've become numb to what *culture change* really means. It's turned into yet another phrase that people throw around carelessly, even when it doesn't really define what's happening. "We're changing our culture. The people from Floor B will now move to Floor C and that will improve our communication exponentially." *Not* culture change. "We're going through a culture change initiative. Our core hours are shifting from 9 AM to 2 PM to 10 AM to 3 PM. This will positively impact our level of customer service." Sorry, not culture change . . . at all. Organizations must begin to recognize the distinction between fake and real culture change—quickly.

This point was underscored in an article in the *Atlantic* called "Why Women Can't Have it All" written last year by Anne-Marie Slaughter, former director of policy planning for the US State Department. After being the first female appointed to the position she held, Slaughter left her high-powered career because she simply wasn't happy. She wasn't able to live the kind of life she wanted, which is what so many people are struggling with today. Slaughter discussed many reasons why it's difficult for women (and we believe men, too) to hold high positions in the workplace (and we would argue more than just "high positions") due to the delicate balance between a work life and a home life.

We experienced many emotions reading the article, especially as we thought about all the women and men whose lives have been completely changed—for the better—as they've transitioned to a ROWE. Women and men who used to wonder how it could all work, or even *if* it could ever all work, and who then find that it can— when the culture is reshaped to manage the work, not the people—enjoy something of an epiphany.

Slaughter cites three "half-truths" that women tell themselves and one another when they talk about both being successful in the workplace and having a great family experience. She relays that many women think that they can have it all if they are *committed* enough, if they *marry the right person*, and if they *sequence their life* in the right order. She goes on to argue that none of these half-truths really work, or even make a lot of sense, in the quest for the perfect work/life balance. She also laments that many women (and again, we would add men here, too) have to choose work or life in the end, painting a pretty bleak picture of the workplace.

She then wrote the four sentences that boil it down crisply and concisely. In the article spread round the world, Slaughter writes:

> I still strongly believe that women can "have it all" (and that men can, too). I believe that we can "have it all at the same time." But not today, not with the way America's economy and society are currently structured. My experiences over the past three years

have forced me to confront a number of uncomfortable facts that need to be widely acknowledged—
and quickly changed.

This is exactly what Jody and I realized many years
ago when we met and spewed into each others' ears all the
things that were "wrong" with the work environment. It's
the *system* that had become dysfunctional, and we weren't
going to sit back and live within a system that strangled the
ability to live the kinds of lives we wanted to live . . . and
as a result, undermine our ability to deliver to the organization we worked for. Selfishly, yes, it was the thought
of wanting to change the system to benefit our own lives
that came to mind first. However, we quickly realized that
we were creating a strategy and process that had the
potential to affect thousands, even millions, of lives around
the globe, and *that* became our mission. It's a mission
that's certainly frustrating at times. For us, it's just common sense that every organization would want to ensure
they are as focused as humanly possible on results. But
that's not always the case.

During a visit I made last year with the students of
the University of Tennessee's Professional MBA Program, the program's director Dr. Michael McIntyre
made this observation: "I think the biggest challenge to
traditional working environments, and what prevents
widespread adoption of a ROWE, is the fact that ROWE
emphasizes personal responsibility. Let's face it; we live
in a society that's not particularly big on personal
responsibility." Well, there's a slap in the face for our

society! But he's right. Dr. McIntyre went on with his examination:

What ROWE expects of the individual:
- Take care of your business—wherever, however, and whenever you need to
- You won't be rewarded for putting in time
- No one is impressed with, or sympathetic to, the amount of time you work
- The only thing you're measured on is your results.

This is the opposite of how a traditional work environment treats its employees. ROWE puts a lot of pressure and personal responsibility on each worker. Most people want credit for effort—"Look how many hours I put in! I worked on this project all weekend!" Yet, if the project isn't finished by deadline, if you do not meet your results, the amount of effort really doesn't matter. It's as if the workforce is still expecting "Participation Awards" that they hand out in elementary school. The wonderful thing about focusing on results is that you no longer have these kinds of ridiculous conversations: "I see you're 10 minutes late," "I see you've taken a lot of time off in the month of June," "Why do you have to leave at 4:30 today?" "No, you can't work from home 2 days a week to save on gas." In a ROWE, you can't be taken to task for anything but the work.

What does ROWE expect from managers?
- Two-way discussions about goals and metrics for everyone on the team.
- Real discussions about performance issues (not just vague directives like, "You need to work harder").

Many managers don't want to have those conversations. They find it very challenging to be involved in goals conversations with team members. Traditional workplace rules have taught managers to manage *people*, but not how to manage the work. [Remember, this is from the director of a Professional MBA Program!]

What does ROWE expect of an organization?

- Meritocracy, not bureaucracy
- Transparency and accountability

This is very healthy for companies. But transparency and accountability also make many people (employees and managers) uncomfortable—especially since a ROWE will inevitably highlight the differences between individuals' ability. Some people will produce results more quickly than others. Consequently, the others will claim that ROWE isn't fair, and conflict-avoiding managers will take their side.

So what are we going to do? My fear is that we will do what we so often do in our society: avoid short-term discomfort and subsequently erode our long-term health. My *hope* is that we will break this destructive cycle. We need to embrace a focus on RESULTS and personal responsibility if we're going to remain competitive as individuals, as organizations, and as a nation.

What's sometimes most difficult for us, and actually pains us the most, is that there's only so much we can say, show, and do to get organizations and managers to understand the benefits of moving into the future. As much as we want to give everyone the "magic pill" that will cure the asshole managers, eradicate archaic company policies from 1964, remove the laws from 1938 that have no place in the twenty-first century, and send out an electric shock when performance isn't the focus, it's just not that easy.

However, what we have that speaks louder than anything *we* could possibly say is the improved performance you've read about in these chapters of organizations that have moved into the new age of management. And if that doesn't speak to you, our best wishes as you become a fatality of the age that is now dead.

And if you're a manager who is feeling that urge to act, we ask—no, we implore—you to imagine a place where:

- People automatically edit their work and remove low-priority tasks.
- You could stay out of your employees' lives and give them total control over their time.
- You monitor the outcomes, not the hallways.
- You don't have to worry about time-off policies, because employees are integrating work and personal pursuits seamlessly every day.
- People, not policies, manage energy so that your workforce is rested and energized instead of burned out and overworked.
- You can expand your workforce's working hours without expanding their hours worked.
- Cross-training happens naturally and teams meet customer needs seamlessly all the time.
- You don't have to worry if the work is getting done; you have ultimate trust in your employees.

- People flex with the needs of the business all the time without regard to time or day.
- Your workforce is proactive rather than reactive.
- You don't have a vacation liability on your books.
- The business advantage isn't about entitlement; it's about opportunity

Our vision remains to make a ROWE the status quo—and with managers who can read the preceding and tap into their passion for making these statements true, it will happen. The question of whether it happens for *you* and *your* organization sooner rather than later sits in your hands.

So, are you focused on what matters?

About the Authors

Cali Ressler and Jody Thompson are the founders of CultureRx, LLC, an organization that offers training services to help organizations adopt an authentic Results-Only Work Environment (ROWE). GPS can usually locate Cali in Minneapolis, where she resides with her husband and four children. Jody mostly rests her head in Chicago with her fiancé and two cats.

Index

'Jesus . . . '

He turned and looked up the block. He saw a dozen people on the sidewalk — mostly strangers, a few familiar faces — but Harry was gone.

★   ★   ★

A cab pulled over at the corner of 110th Street and Malcolm X Boulevard. Harry got out and walked into the north end of Central Park. The waters of the Harlem Meer were still and slate gray; half a dozen mallards paddled about aimlessly near the shore.

Harry hobbled down the walk, giving way to the rollerbladers and skateboarders. The ghosts followed him wherever he went — there had been no bodies to identify, there were no fresh graves and etched headstones — and he could not lay them to rest. He was a shepherd of the dead: Geiger, though a peripheral presence, was always nearby, but it was Lily who Harry kept closest to him. The concept of his sister's death was still entirely abstract. Her sudden and complete absence from his life had tipped its scales out of balance, and the fact that he would never see her again was unacceptable. His dreams overflowed with the giddy laughter and rituals of children. His grief was exhausting and perpetual.

He sat on a bench facing the lake.

'Harry?' the man next to him said.

'Sorry I'm late,' Harry said, turning to shake David Matheson's extended hand.

'Good to meet you finally.'

Harry glanced at Matheson and then looked away. He put the cane between his legs and toggled it back and forth by the handle, another new habit.

'Tell me, Harry. How did you figure out 'BigBossMan'?'

Harry shrugged. 'I was able to get into Geiger's IMs. Through my PC.'

'Really? That's pretty tough to do.'

'Took a while. But I've got some programs I cooked up.'

Out of the corner of his eye, Harry saw a figure running toward him. He stiffened, his hands tightening on the cane, but then settled back when the jogger ran by.

'How's Ezra?' he said.

'Beginning to work through things, but still not in great shape. I've only seen him once — secretly, and just for a few hours at a hotel with his mother. It's not fair for me to be around him much with all the heat on me now. I'm never in one place more than a day or two. Anyway, he says he's playing a lot of violin. I guess that's a good thing.'

'I guess,' Harry said. 'Tell me something, Matheson. Were you ever in the art business?'

'No. That was just a cover so I could move around.'

Harry quickly surveyed his surroundings and then took a small package from a pocket. 'I found a way to open the digital lock, so now you've got the originals and two copies.'

'Much appreciated,' Matheson said. He took

And, most especially, Nat Sobel and Judith Weber, my agents and friends, who thought that there was something worthwhile about this book, and, in so doing, changed my life. While writing the five additional drafts Nat demanded, it became clear to me that (at least) one of the reasons he was drawn to the book was his affinity for the black art performed within its pages. In turning my manuscript into a novel, Nat was my tireless mentor, ruthless editor, and torturous taskmaster — and I thank him deeply for his passion, faith, and wisdom.

Acknowledgments

I consider myself immeasurably blessed to have so many people to thank:

Stephen Rubin, publisher and president of Henry Holt, for reading this book and deciding that others should have an opportunity to do the same.

John Sterling, my editor, for his skill and dedication, his imagination and diligence, and his honesty.

Andre Bernard, friend and scholar, who, in a very real sense, made this all happen, and to whom I shall be forever grateful.

Cari-Esta Albert, the true-bluest pal, critic, confidant, and sounding board on this tiny planet, and Susan Brecker, whose love, strength, and support are treasures.

Liz Robinson and Dodie Gold, best of managers and dearest of friends, for their guidance and loyalty all these many years.

Drs. Robert Zevin and Lawrence Weisberg and Jaine O'Neill, for always taking the time to let me pick their wise brains about bodies and minds.

Luis Rumbaut, for his tireless, dead-on translations.

Dr. Andrew C. Lotterman, whose insight and care helped me see what it was I was really trying to write, and *why*.

recognized the man. He wore black-framed glasses, and curls spilled out from under a back-turned baseball cap. A trim black beard reached almost to his cheekbones.

In his hand the man held a dusty, palm-sized portion of broken flooring. He wiped it clean on his pants and studied it: the fragment was made of mahogany, with an ash inlay of a crescent moon. Holding it with his fingertips, he turned it twenty degrees clockwise, then twenty degrees back the other way, as one might do with a piece of a jigsaw puzzle that was not yet part of the whole.

'*The world knows nothing of you. That is my gift to you. You are no one.*'

The man slid the piece of wood into his pocket, picked up the cat, and perched the animal on his shoulder.

'Time to go,' he said.

He got to his feet slowly, turned, and started across the foundation toward the sidewalk. He had a slight limp, but somehow the man incorporated it into the swing of his body as he moved.

One could say it lent him a certain measure of grace.

the package and slid it into a small bag on the bench next to him. 'You're very good at what you do, Harry.'

'Thanks.'

'In fact, Veritas Arcana could really use someone with your skills. We're getting bigger every day — four servers now, all over the globe — but those who don't like what we do are always breathing down our necks, trying to shut us down.'

'I don't think so, man. Sorry.'

'Well, think about it. If you change your mind, you obviously won't have any trouble finding me.'

★　★　★

The eastern horizon showed the faintest illumination, a preface to dawn.

Atop the back fence that had been fashioned into a miniature skyline, a cat appeared. After walking a few feet along the jagged edge, the cat jumped down into the yard.

All that was left of the structure that had once occupied the lot was the cleared foundation and its concrete stoop in back. The cat went up the two steps, lay down on the stoop, and began to lick himself clean from his night's labors.

At the sound of uneven footsteps, the cat looked up. A man sat down on the stoop and began scratching the scar above the the cat's eyeless socket. The cat responded with a rumbling purr.

No one from the neighborhood would have